OSPREY
PUBLISHING

US Army Ranger 1983–2002

Sua Sponte – Of their own accord

Mir Bahmanyar • Illustrated by Michael Welply

First published in Great Britain in 2003 by Osprey Publishing,
Midland House, West Way, Botley, Oxford OX2 0PH, UK
443 Park Avenue South, New York, NY 10016, USA

E-mail: info@ospreypublishing.com

A CIP catalog record for this book is available from the British Library

ISBN 1 84603 010 2

Editor: Tom Lowres
Design: Ken Vail Graphic Design, Cambridge, UK
Index by Alan Rutter
Originated by Grasmere Digital Imaging, Leeds, UK
Printed in China through World Print Ltd.

05 06 07 08 09   10 9 8 7 6 5 4 3 2 1

FOR A CATALOG OF ALL BOOKS PUBLISHED BY OSPREY
MILITARY AND AVIATION PLEASE CONTACT:

NORTH AMERICA
Osprey Direct, 2427 Bond Street, University Park, IL 60466, USA
E-mail: info@ospreydirectusa.com

ALL OTHER REGIONS
Osprey Direct UK, P.O. Box 140 Wellingborough, Northants, NN8 2FA, UK
E-mail: info@ospreydirect.co.uk

Buy online at **www.ospreypublishing.com**

Artist's note

Readers may care to note that the original paintings from
which the color plates in this book were prepared are
available for private sale. All reproduction copyright
whatsoever is retained by the Publishers. All enquiries
should be addressed to:

michael.welply@wanadoo.fr

The Publishers regret that they can enter into no
correspondence upon this matter.

Acknowledgments

Special thanks to Sara van Valkenburg, Rangers Berendsen,
Collett and a special HOOAH to Ranger/Fallschirmjäger
Johannes Galetzka and Ranger "Chickenfarmer." Carol
Darby, USASOC Public Affairs, and the Rangers at 2/75
Public Affairs.

FRONT COVER **A Ranger carrying an M-4 carbine runs
to the objective during a training exercise. Behind him,
another Ranger provides covering fire with a .50 caliber
mounted machine gun on top of a Ranger Special
Operations Vehicle (RSOV). He is completely exposed to
potential enemy fire. Attempts to create a protective shield
for the gunner have failed as they make the RSOV too
top-heavy. (Nancy Fisher, USASOC)**

CONTENTS

US ARMY RANGER 1983–2002

INTRODUCTION

Acknowledging the fact that a Ranger is a more elite soldier . . .

Rangers have attained a near-legendary status within the hierarchy of the United States Army. No other unit can point to as colorful or impressive a combat record. The reputation of these hardened soldiers, seemingly impervious to fire and ice, has been earned over centuries on the world's most challenging battlefields. "I wanna be an Airborne-Ranger" is the first stanza of the most famous of all US Army cadences, homage to the few men who wear the distinctive Ranger scroll on their uniform. Yet, despite their elite reputation, Ranger units have consistently been disbanded after each war, only to be reactivated during subsequent periods of military need.

The modern-day 75th Ranger Regiment traces its history as far back as Robert Rogers' Rangers of the French-Indian Wars (1754–63) and Ranger Francis Marion of the Revolutionary War (1775–83). Indeed, Rangers were so popular that hundreds of northern and southern units carried that prestigious title during the American Civil War (1861–65). It was not until the maelstrom of the Second World War (1939–45) that Ranger units were again formed. The 1st, 2nd, 3rd, 4th, 5th Ranger Battalions and the 29th Rangers saw action in Europe, while the 6th Ranger Battalion served with distinction in the Pacific. The same region produced the 5307th Composite Unit Provisional (CUP), commonly known as Merrill's Marauders. The unit became the 475th Infantry and

Secretary of Defense, Donald Rumsfeld, with 2/75 Rangers at Fort Bragg, North Carolina in December 2001. Note the new Kevlar MICH (Modular/Integrated Communications Helmet) helmets with mounted night vision devices (NODS), starched uniforms and modular load-bearing equipment. Of particular interest are the helmet straps for airborne operations as worn by the Ranger in the middle of the photograph. (DOD)

was finally designated as the 75th Infantry. The first airborne-qualified Ranger companies were founded during the Korean War (1950–53), but they, too, were disbanded at the end of the war. The tradition of "ranging" excellence was continued during the United States' longest conflict, the Vietnam War (1956–75). By 1968, Long Range Patrol (LRP) and Long Range Reconnaissance Patrol (LRRP) units were transformed into Ranger companies. By the end of the war, almost every Ranger company had been deactivated.

In 1974 the Department of the Army decided that the United States needed a force that could rapidly deploy worldwide, and two Ranger units, Companies A and B, 75th Infantry (Ranger) provided the backbone of this force, the 1st and 2nd Battalion (Ranger), 75th Infantry. General Creighton Abrams, Army Chief of Staff and veteran tank commander of World War II, was the impetus behind the creation of the first battalion-sized Ranger units since 1945. He believed a tough and disciplined Ranger unit would set a high standard for the rest of the Army and that their influence would improve the entire Army. The Abrams Charter stipulated, "the Ranger Battalion to be an elite, light, and the most proficient infantry battalion in the world; a battalion that can do things with its hands and weapons better than anyone. The Battalion will contain no hoodlums or brigands and that if the battalion were formed of such, it should be disbanded. Wherever the Ranger Battalion goes, it is apparent that it is the best."

On January 25, 1974, Headquarters, United States Army Forces Command, published General Orders 127, directing the activation of the 1st Battalion (Ranger), 75th

These Long Range Reconnaissance Patrollers and Rangers (LRRP/LRP/Ranger) contributed significantly to the history and lineage of the 75th Ranger Regiment. Operating in small teams, they wreaked havoc in enemy-held territories. (Pat Tadina)

Rangers at Fort Lewis with Mount Rainier in the background. Barely visible are the ALICE rucksacks on their 15-foot lowering lines. (John Galetzka)

Infantry, with an effective date of January 31, 1974. On July 1, 1974, the 1st Battalion (Ranger), 75th Infantry, parachuted into Fort Stewart, Georgia. The 2nd Battalion (Ranger), 75th Infantry was activated shortly thereafter, on October 1, 1974. These units eventually established their headquarters at Hunter Army Airfield, Georgia, and Fort Lewis, Washington, respectively.

The modern Ranger battalions were first called to arms in 1980. Elements of 1st Battalion, 75th Infantry (Ranger) participated in Operation Eagle Claw, the ill-fated Iranian hostage rescue attempt. The United States' invasion of Grenada on October 25, 1983 was codenamed Operation Urgent Fury, with the Rangers tasked to protect the lives of American citizens and to restore democracy to the island. The 1st and 2nd (-) Ranger Battalions conducted a low-level parachute assault from 500 feet, seized the airfield at Point Salinas, rescued American citizens at the True Blue Medical Campus, and conducted follow-on air assault operations. Eight Rangers were killed in action: Randy E. Cline, Phillip S. Grenier, Kevin J. Lannon, Markin R. Maynard, Mark A. Rademacher, Russell L. Robinson, Stephen E. Slater, Mark O. Yamane.

The 75th Ranger Regiment
The exceptional reputation of the Rangers led to the creation of a third battalion and a Regimental Headquarters, both provisionally designated on July 1, 1984 with an effective date of October 3, 1984 at Fort Benning, Georgia, the Home of the Infantry. By February 2, 1986, the 75th Ranger Regiment was officially awarded the lineage and honors of all previous Ranger units. The current 75th Ranger Regiment, composed of a headquarters and headquarters company, as well as three infantry battalions, holds in its ranks fewer than 2,000 Rangers. It is an all-male, homogeneous, strictly hierarchical and severely disciplined combat unit, complete with its own rituals and idiosyncrasies.

The 75th Ranger Regiment plans and conducts conventional and special military operations in support of US foreign policy. The

The flash affixed to the black beret worn by all members of the 75th Ranger Regiment was designed by the 1st Battalion's Command Sergeant-Major, Neal Gentry, in 1974. The colors (white, green, blue, orange, khaki, and red) represent the six original combat team colors of Merrill's Marauders. (Author's collection)

cornerstone of Ranger missions is that of direct action, specifically, airfield seizures and raids. Ranger units conduct training that includes movement-to-contact, ambush, reconnaissance, airborne and air assaults, hasty defense, infiltrating and exfiltrating by land, sea, and air, as well as the recovery of personnel and special equipment. A typical Ranger battalion mission involves seizing an airfield for use by follow-on, general purpose forces (GPF) and conducting raids on key targets of operational or strategic importance. Having no armor, Rangers rely heavily on external fire support.

A squad in highly starched and extremely popular Vietnam-era OG 107 jungle fatigues. These uniforms were worn until the late 1980s when the regiment changed to the woodland pattern battle dress uniform. Rangers referred to the new uniforms derogatorily as "duckhunters." (Author's collection)

Rangers using a "sand table" detailing their objective. Meticulous planning is the key to Ranger success and every Ranger is involved in the process. Ranger training requires every man to be completely knowledgeable of the task at hand. (John Galetzka)

Regimental Headquarters consists of a Command Group, a signal (communications) detachment (RSD – Regimental Signal Detachment), a fire support element, a reconnaissance detachment (RRD – Regimental Reconnaissance Detachment), a cadre for the Ranger Training Detachment (RTD), and a Company Headquarters. The RTD is responsible for running the Ranger Indoctrination Program (RIP), a three-week selection course for new recruits; the Ranger Orientation Program (ROP), a two-week program for Rangers returning to the Regiment; and lastly, Pre-Ranger, a three-week course to prepare Rangers for the US Army Ranger School. Ranger School is a 58-day leadership course run by the School of Infantry's Ranger Training Brigade (RTB), not the 75th Ranger Regiment.

The three Ranger battalions are identical in organization. Each battalion consists of three rifle companies and a headquarters and headquarters company (HHC). Each battalion is authorized 580 Rangers, although an additional 15 percent of personnel are allotted to make allowances for Rangers attending military schools. Each battalion must be able to deploy anywhere in the world within 18 hours notice. Ranger battalions are light infantry and have only a few vehicles and crew-served weapons systems. They operate a minimum of anti-aircraft and anti-armor weapons. Rangers can deploy for only a few days at a time as they lack the inherent support needed for longer operations.

The three rifle companies are each assigned 152 Rangers. Their organization reflects that of the battalion, each comprising a headquarters and headquarters element, three rifle platoons, and a weapons platoon. The weapons platoon of each rifle company contains a mortar section, an anti-tank/armor section and a sniper section.

The battalions alternate as the unit on Ready Reaction Force (RRF) 1, the force able to deploy within 18 hours of notification. RRF1 rotates between the three battalions, normally in 13-week periods. While on RRF1, the designated battalion is prohibited from conducting any off-post training or deployments to ensure that they can meet the required deployment time standards. Additionally, one rifle company with battalion command and control must be able to deploy within nine hours. The Regimental Headquarters remains on RRF1 at all times.

Today's Rangers are encouraged to experiment with personal gear as long as it makes tactical sense. Notice the different modular attachments to the Ranger Body Armor (RBA). Also note the green socks on the goggles' retaining bands used to prevent "sparkle" when worn on the Kevlar helmet. The sock slides over the goggles. The MICH helmets are so new that few have camouflage covers. (Justin Viene, 2/75 PAO)

A fine photo of a weapons squad from 1989–90. The Ranger on the far right wears "stereo scrolls." A scroll on the right shoulder indicates combat status. His unit scroll is on the left side. (Author's collection)

The entire Ranger regiment participated in Operation Just Cause, in which US forces restored democracy to Panama. Rangers spearheaded the action on December 20, 1989 by conducting two important operations. The 1st Battalion, reinforced by Company C, 3rd Battalion, and a regimental command and control team, conducted an early morning parachute assault onto Omar Torrijos International Airport and Tocumen Military Airfield. Their mission was to neutralize the Panamanian Defense Force (PDF) 2nd Rifle Company, as well as the entire Panamanian Air Force. They were also tasked with securing the airfields for the arrival of the 82nd Airborne Division. The 2nd and 3rd (-) Ranger Battalions, in conjunction with a regimental command and control team, conducted a parachute assault onto the airfield at Rio Hato to neutralize PDF 6th and 7th Rifle Companies and also seized General Manuel Noriega's beach house. After the successful completion of these assaults, Rangers conducted follow-on operations. The Rangers sustained five killed: Larry Barnard, Roy Brown, Jr., Philip Lear, James W. Markwell, and John Price.

Rangers from the 1st Battalion, 75th Ranger Regiment deployed to Saudi Arabia from February 12 to April 6, 1991, in support of Operation Desert Storm. Company B and elements from Company A, 1st Battalion, 75th Ranger Regiment conducted raids and were employed as a quick reaction force for Allied units. In December 1991, 1/75 and the Regimental Headquarters deployed to Kuwait in a show of force called Operation Iris Gold. The Rangers performed a daylight airborne assault onto Ali Al Salem airfield, near Kuwait City, conducted a 50-km foot march and a live fire exercise. For this action, the battalion was awarded the Southwest Asia Service Medal (SWASM) with bronze campaign star. Rangers sustained no casualties in these operations.

From August 26, 1993 to October 21, 1993, Company B and a command and control element of 3rd Battalion, 75th Ranger Regiment, in conjunction with C Squadron, 1st Special Forces Operational Detachment – Delta (SFOD-D), deployed to Somalia in Operation

Gothic Serpent to capture key leaders in the city of Mogadishu. Six Rangers were killed in action: James M. Cavaco, James C. Joyce, Richard W. Kowalewski, Dominick M. Pilla, Lorenzo M. Ruiz, and James E. Smith.

In October 2001, the 75th Ranger Regiment deployed its battalions to participate in Operation Enduring Freedom. Two combat parachute assaults were conducted against Taliban-held airfields in Afghanistan, along with numerous clandestine special operations missions. The Rangers have suffered five killed in the ongoing campaign. From the 1st Battalion, 75th Ranger Regiment, Bradley Crose, Marc Anderson, and Matthew Commons; from the 3rd Ranger Battalion, John Edmunds and Kristofor Stonesifer.

CHRONOLOGY

July 1, 1974	Formation of 1st Battalion (Ranger), 75th Infantry.
October 1, 1974	Formation of 2nd Battalion (Ranger), 75th Infantry.
April 20, 1980	Operation Eagle Claw, the Iranian hostage rescue attempt.
October 25, 1983	Operation Urgent Fury, the invasion of Grenada.
October 3, 1984	Formation of 3rd Battalion and Regimental Headquarters.
February 2, 1986	75th Ranger Regiment officially awarded the lineage and honors of older Ranger units.
December 20, 1989	Operation Just Cause, the invasion of Panama.
February 12, 1991	Operation Desert Storm in Saudi Arabia.
August 26, 1993	Operation Gothic Serpent in Somalia.
June 14, 2001	Black beret adopted by regular army, Rangers change to tan beret.
July 27, 2001	75th Ranger Regiment's official ceremony donning the tan beret.
October 2001	Operation Enduring Freedom in Afghanistan.
2002 – on-going	US Forces are still hunting for al Qaueda and Taleban fighters in Afghanistan in the wake of the September 11 terror attacks on the United States

VOLUNTEERING

Recognizing that I volunteered as a Ranger . . .

The Basics

Rangers are four-time volunteers: the army, airborne, service with the Ranger Regiment and finally, Ranger School. The sheer fortitude required to endure the harsh mental and physical requirements leaves many hopeful young men stranded by the wayside, failing in one way or another to meet the high Ranger standard. The following narrative represents the composite experience of a young man becoming a United States Army Ranger between the years of 1985–95. Although the weapons and equipment may have changed somewhat, the core of the experience is still very much the same.

Men are drawn to elite units for many reasons. Some join for financial considerations, others enlist for the adventure or to find structure in life. But no matter the reason for enlistment, all of them strive to be the best. And in the United States Army, the Rangers are the best. In this case, the civilian wants to join the Rangers since his father served as one in Vietnam. Having been raised with a sense of duty and respect for his father, it was an easy choice to make. In order to join the military, the recruit must pass a battery of tests. His local recruiter schedules a medical examination and written test at local facilities. Upon passing these and informing the recruiter that he wants to go to a Ranger unit, the young man is guaranteed, in writing, an opportunity to try out. He signs a contract for a four-year tour of duty and is told that failing any one part of the training will render his contract ineffectual, whereupon the army, at its discretion, may assign him anywhere in the world.

A Special Forces Command officer describes the exercise to President George W. Bush at Fort Bragg, North Carolina, March 2002. On the right is a Ranger officer from 2/75. Note the MH-47, a heavy helicopter used extensively during Operation Enduring Freedom in Afghanistan as an equipment and troop transport. (DOD)

The recruit is then flown on a civilian airliner to Atlanta, Georgia where a drill sergeant will place him and the other recruits on buses for the journey to Fort Benning, Georgia for basic and advanced individual training. Basic training lasts 8 weeks and AIT (Advanced Individual Training) for the infantry is another 4 weeks. There he is taught rudimentary soldiering skills. After successful completion of the 12-week training, he begins the 3-week airborne training, a requirement for all Ranger hopefuls. Finally, he attempts to pass the selection course for Rangers, the Ranger Indoctrination Program. Upon graduation and after arrival at RIP, he may spend 2–4 weeks as a "holdover" before his RIP course begins. If the recruit should fail, he may be given another opportunity to start over with the next class, but this is at the discretion and needs of the Army.

Fresh from basic, the soldier begins his three-week stint at the US Army Airborne School at Fort Benning, Georgia. Students begin every morning with the airborne-shuffle, a slow and steady jog, and today they pass by the old World War II Jump School barracks that house the 75th Ranger Regiment's Ranger Indoctrination Program. Somberly called RIP, it is a three-week course on Ranger skills designed to weed out the weak. [In the mid-1990s the program moved to the Ranger Regiment's Headquarters compound.] The recruit, having heard stories of the difficult Ranger training while at basic training, gawks in fear and admiration at the soldiers who have already earned their jump wings and are now testing their mettle at the much more arduous selection course. He still has weeks to go before going to RIP and this is the first time he has seen any Ranger students. The "Rippies" lean forward to compensate for their extremely heavy rucksacks, their faces bearing camouflage paint in the prescribed regimental fashion of a tiger stripe pattern. It is an imposing sight. The airborne student, going to RIP in a few weeks, has many questions on his mind: "Is it true that Rangers hit each other in the face?" "Can I carry that rucksack?"

The three weeks quickly pass by and Airborne School graduation has a few memorable moments including the "Blood Wings" ceremony. "Blood wings" are given by removing the back plates of the sharp pins, then placing the points above the graduate's left breast pocket and sending them home, into the chest, with a resounding thud by a fist or palm. Prior to graduation, Ranger-contracted students are assembled and jogged over to an empty building. Here, the RIP Cadre explains the hardships of training and the demanding life of an Airborne Ranger.

A maggot machine gunner showing the strains of infantry work in heavy jungles. A blank adapter for the M-60 is mounted to the front of the barrel. (John Galetzka)

They advise the recruits to leave while they can if this lifestyle is not for them. It is eerie when by the time the cadre finishes the speech more than half of the 40 men quit and leave for reassignment. Those who remain are told to have fresh Ranger haircuts, the "high-and-tight", by next day's formation.

The Ranger Cadre, the training staff, is usually excellent. Supreme samples of physical prowess coupled with years of service at a Ranger battalion make for extremely motivated and dedicated individuals. No matter the verbal and physical abuse, recruits are treated with respect. The cadre addresses them as Rangers. Unlike other units in the army where encouragement is the modus operandi, Rangers are always asked to re-evaluate their motivation. The sole purpose of the Ranger Indoctrination Program is to make the individual quit. There is no encouragement to stay.

The day after graduation, 20 Ranger recruits wait at Airborne School for the RIP Cadre to arrive, knowing nothing except that Rangers are hard-core, mean and scary individuals. The cadre arrives with one bus on to which the men and gear are loaded and then driven the short distance to the RIP compound.

Ranger Indoctrination Program (RIP)

The airborne graduates pile out of the bus onto the Red Square, a red clay field between the old Jump School barracks. The recruits' first acquaintance with a Ranger "smoke session" (tough physical exercise) starts immediately. It is here that they become familiar with elevated Ranger push-ups, or more precisely, "the front, lean and rest position... move! One, two, three... one, two, three... recover!" Verbal abuse is constant. The recruit low crawls around the entire Red Square, giving him an intimate appreciation of Georgia's red clay. Slowly, the recruit drags his body across Mother Earth, while highly motivated Ranger instructors hurl verbal abuse and, occasionally, help grind his face deeper into the ground by placing a boot on the back of his head. Next, the Rangers assume the flutter-kick position on their backs, their hands underneath the small of the back, chin to chest and feet 12 inches off the ground. It is a four-count exercise, each leg has to conduct scissors-like movements twice before one count is completed. The instructors are not opposed to stepping on the recruit's stomach as he does the exercise.

The Headshed, the headquarters building of RIP, has a fake grave in front of its main entrance. A tombstone reads "Rest In Peace" and the Cadre tells the Rippies that there "lies a Ranger who did not listen carefully to instructions and got himself killed." Nearby is the facility that issues Rangers their gear for training: helmets, web gear and rucksacks.

The recruits are housed in the beaten-up World War II barracks, where the facilities are Spartan at best. A handful of toilets and a couple of nozzles serve as the bathing facilities for 50 men. Cockroaches nearly the size of field mice frequently scurry about the showering area. Life as a "holdover", an individual waiting to start the next class, takes its toll. More than a few soldiers quit, each with his own legitimate reason. Weeks may pass before a new RIP class begins as the instructors wait to amass enough volunteers to warrant a new course. Class sizes vary, but can be as low as 50 or as high as 200.

The recruit begins his RIP class with 68 men and is determined to succeed and make his father proud. The Rippies are given an introduction to the standards required to graduate the class and learn the Ranger motto of *Sua Sponte*, Latin for "of their own accord," inspired by the long history of the Ranger volunteer.

The typical Ranger has to complete many tasks: daily physical training (falling out of runs will incur the wrath of the Cadre); a Ranger history test has to be passed with a 70% score; map reading; airborne operations; day and night land navigation; a five-mile run with a time of at least eight minutes per mile; combatives (hand-to-hand combat); knots; a Combat Water Survival Test (CWST) complete with boots and LBE (Load Bearing Equipment); six-, eight- and 10-mile road marches; driver training; fast rope training; and Combat Lifesaver certification.

The class is divided into squads, and squad leaders, based on seniority, are assigned. Dismissed on a Friday afternoon with RIP scheduled to begin the following Monday, they are reminded that they are not allowed to leave the RIP compound. As Saturday morning rolls around and the recruits are hanging around the barracks, a bored Cadre member calls the Rippies to formation and takes them on a five-mile run around the adjacent airfield.

All Rangers sound off with "Hooah!" Everything is answered with a resounding, at times, blood-curdling scream of "Hooah, Sergeant!" It could mean anything, but "Hooah" is foremost a Ranger

The latrines at RIP (Ranger Indoctrination Program). The WWII Jump School barracks were ideal for housing students as the emphasis was on training and not barracks maintenance. (Author's collection)

The Pit at RIP is visible to the right. In the background are cargo nets and rope climbing structures. The Headshed was off to the left. Barely visible in the foreground is one of the barracks buildings. This facility was destroyed in the mid 1990s when RIP moved to the regiment's headquarters compound. (Author's collection)

term, no matter that its use has become fashionable with the regular army. A typical conversation would go something like this: "You hate me, doncha Ranga?" "Hooah, Sergeant!" Amused, the instructor would shout with plenty of expletives, "Stop eyeballing me. You better beat your face till I get tired, Ranger."

First Call on Monday morning at RIP is marked with Cadre running into the barracks at 0430, banging loudly on garbage cans and tossing a few sleepy students onto the floor. The class drops a number of students who fail to pass the minimum physical fitness test given that morning. Ranger recruits perform push-ups and sit-ups, each within a two-minute time limit. To pass they will have to achieve a minimum of 42 push-ups and 52 sit-ups. A two-mile run has to be completed within 16 minutes as well. Ranger push-ups require the chest to touch the ground and fast push-ups are not allowed. The head has to be up and facing forward as well. Each push-up must be precise – a recruit might complete 70 or 80 push-ups but will receive no credit if his form is deemed incorrect.

The Pit, a round sandbagged enclosure filled with sawdust, is the site of more push-ups and other physical training. Some slow-moving students low-crawl with sandbags on their backs. Water, sprayed maliciously from a hose, makes low-crawling that much more difficult. The class is divided into two-man groups in the pit. A Ranger instructor shouts with precision and the utmost professionalism, "Number One man, take sawdust in your hand and stick it down Number Two man's crotch." Minutes go by as the rage in Number Two man boils and then, "Number One man, hit Number Two man in the face (open palm)." Although combatives varied over the years, from Judo to the current grappling techniques, the purpose is to instill confidence and controlled aggression into the Rangers.

Men are hurt on occasion and will need the attention of a nearby medic. A couple of broken bones or sprains will further reduce the class. Such injuries are frowned upon by the officer hierarchy, and from time to time hand-to-hand combat has been eliminated from the Ranger Indoctrination Program.

The swim test is a reasonably straightforward affair. A rubber version of the M-16 rifle, a set of LBE (Load Bearing Equipment) composed of a pistol belt, shoulder straps, ammunition pouches and boots complete the uniform for the test. The students climb a three-meter springboard, are blindfolded and walk off the tower. They must retain control of their weapons while landing and then successfully swim to the edge of the swimming pool. After that, the students must swim 15 meters and conduct an underwater removal of their LBE. More losses are incurred by the group.

Ruck-running (running while carrying the issue rucksack) is strictly forbidden in the modern military as it causes serious injuries to the joints. Nonetheless, it is a part of the modern soldier's life, and in this RIP class a five-mile ruck-run to the Rappel towers is a real smoker. The ruck run is composed of two distinct parts: running and speed walking. The class runs a few hundred meters, then speed-walks for another couple of hundred meters, repeating this pattern for five miles. More people quit.

Students who quit or fail are sent to other units in need of personnel. Occasionally, the RIP quitters end up at the Ranger Training Brigade, the outfit responsible for Ranger School. Some of them graduate Ranger School and may end up at a Ranger battalion in their second term of enlistment.

Down the ravine between the old RIP compound and the airfield is an obstacle course named the "Downing Mile" after a popular Ranger officer, and it is regularly used by the RIP students. Rope climbing, cargo nets, commando ropes and other obstacles make for excellent exercise and are great confidence builders.

After nearly three weeks, the class is down to 50 students. The last requirement is to complete a 12-mile road march with at least 45lb in the rucksack. The Rippies are worried as they know that previous classes have had a high fallout rate. The summers in Georgia are hot and humid and pre-hydration is key. Supposed miracle drinks, like "Rocket Fuel", are taken by some, others gulp mass quantities of popular sports drinks, while some stick to plain old water. A few go so far as to quietly have a medic in the class administer intravenous fluids.

The RIP class packs their rucksacks and makes sure they weigh more than the required 45lb. The Cadre has told them that the rucks will be weighed after the march and anyone caught with less than the mandatory weight will have to retake the road march the very same or next day. At 0330 on a Thursday morning the RIP class moves out with two lines on each side of the road. As the march continues, more and more students fall out, twist an ankle or collapse from heat exhaustion, sometimes called the "Kicking Chicken." RIP instructors with ambulances follow the formation and collect fallen Rangers by the wagon load. Three hours and 12 miles later, seven individuals cross the finish line as a group with just seconds to spare. A few stragglers complete the march but do not pass as they failed to finish with the group. Rucks are weighed, averaging 52lb. Utterly exhausted, the survivors take long showers and prepare for their out-processing. Graduation is tomorrow. Others are given the opportunity to retake the 12 miler that day or very early the next morning. A 50 percent fallout rate is common. This particular class graduates less than a dozen out of 68.

RIP Graduation

The RIP graduate calls his father with the good news. He is proud as is his family. A long tradition of excellence has passed onto the new generation. The new Ranger is ordered to his unit, the 2nd Ranger Battalion at Fort Lewis, Washington. Other graduates are assigned to other Ranger battalions and a few have orders to go to the Regimental Headquarters just a short distance away. The assignments vary depending on the needs of each unit.

That afternoon the new graduates buy Ranger coins, each specific to their new units, and the highly coveted black Ranger Beret (on June 14, 2001 the 75th Ranger Regiment switched to a tan beret as the entire US Army adopted the black beret). From now on, each Ranger will carry his coin wherever he goes. Failure to furnish the coin when "coin-checked", (challenged by any Ranger) will result in push-ups or drinks owed. Ranger scrolls are sewn on several sets of uniforms. The RIP graduate has become a "Scrolled Ranger," having earned the right to wear the Ranger scroll, the unit patch.

Behind the barracks and near the Pit, graduates perform the 15-count manual of arms, a ceremonial precision drill with the M-16 rifle. They don the highly coveted Ranger beret, carefully prepared the night before with instructions from some of the Cadre. After the short ceremony a great sense of accomplishment floods the newly qualified Rangers, although some of the Cadre chuckle at the ignorance of the new "Battboys" – as Rangers from the Ranger battalions are called. But then again, the graduates are young, dumb and full of it, just like the Ranger instructors themselves a few years ago. It is only once the inexperienced Ranger arrives at his Ranger battalion that he learns that Ranger is spelled P-A-I-N, because that is where the real rangering begins.

RIP graduates are wearing BDUs and black berets, while other students, considered worthy, wait to be recycled to the next class to try again. In the background, wearing jungle fatigues and berets, are RIP Cadre. The Georgia clay is red and this area was known as the Red Square. (Author's collection)

APPEARANCE, CLOTHING, EQUIPMENT AND WEAPONS

My neatness of dress and care of equipment shall set the example for others to follow.

When a trainee enters the US Army, he receives various uniforms and gear common to the infantryman. Upon arrival at a Ranger battalion, the soldier is issued specialty equipment needed for the variety of training missions that he is tasked with. Over the years, Rangers have always received the newest and best equipment.

Ranger uniforms have varied from the Vietnam-era camouflage leaf pattern, to the olive green, Army shade 107 (OG-107) jungle fatigues, to the current woodland or desert pattern BDUs (Battle Dress Uniform). The typical Ranger in garrison today wears a tan beret atop his "high-and-tight" haircut. His uniform includes a set of BDUs in the woodland pattern, a set of dog-tags, silenced with tape, underneath his brown T-shirt and a black canvas belt with a black metal buckle. Rangers do not wear underwear and the uniform is so exceptionally well starched, that the Ranger has to break the starch in order to put it on. On his feet he wears green wool socks and spit-shined Vietnam-era jungle boots. On his left arm he wears the subdued Ranger Scroll, inherited from the Rangers of the Second World War, indicating his battalion or regimental affiliation. The Ranger coin is kept easily accessible in one of his pockets. It is always a great feeling to strut around an army post as a Ranger. The chest sticks out further, and the swagger is unmistakable. The army "legs," a term used to describe regular soldiers, both hate and worship him. Or at least so it seems.

The load-bearing equipment (LBE or LCE, load-carrying equipment) has also changed with the times. Rangers currently wear a combination of modular systems known as the RACK (Ranger Assault Carrying Kit) and MOLLE (Modular Lightweight Load-carrying Equipment) and may customize it, unlike their predecessors who wore highly standardized web gear. The traditional LCE (1974–late 1990s) is made up of a pistol belt with either a plastic or metal clasping device: a nylon Y-shaped harness; two one-quart canteens; two ammo pouches; a lensatic compass pouch; and a first-aid pouch. A strobe light pouch may be attached to one of the harness straps, and bayonet or pistol holster might complete the set, depending on the mission.

All gear is securely fastened with green "100-mile per hour" tape and 550-cord. 550-cord looks like a miniature version of a Kernmantel rope: small strands of white nylon surrounded by a green cover with the approximate thickness of a bootlace, with the nylon ends melted to prevent them from unraveling. Theoretically, it can secure anything up to 550lb and, together with the tape, is invaluable to the Ranger for securing his equipment. For example, the hooks of the harness are fastened to the pistol belt, then completely covered with green tape to prevent them from accidentally unhooking. The ammunition pouches are held in place by blackened metal fasteners and then likewise secured to the belt with a piece of 550-cord. In the event that the metal clasps fall off or break, the 550-cord will keep the pouch attached to the belt. The

A Ranger with new tan-colored beret. On the left shoulder is the Ranger tab and below it, the highly coveted Ranger Scroll. Also visible above the US Army nametag are airborne wings and the Expert Infantryman's Badge. (DOD)

entire LBE is secured following the rigid guidelines established by the Ranger Regiment's SOPs (Standard Operating Procedures). Even the black canteen caps are tied down to the canteen with cord and black tape to match the color of the canteen caps.

A rucksack is a Ranger's lifeline. In it he carries everything he needs, from clothing to food to ammunition. The current rucksack of choice is the large-sized, three-pouch, ALICE (All-purpose Light Individual Carrying Equipment). A two-quart canteen on one side and an E-tool (entrenching tool) on the other are securely fastened with black metal clasps, tape and cord and are further held in place with an airborne strap. The ALICE has an external steel frame for support, and the belt is permanently removed from the ruck. The top of the frame is covered with various colored tapes to identify the company. A name tag and cat's eyes on top of the flap of the rucksack, complete the ALICE.

As Rangers are issued numerous items to equip them for all types of terrain, from jungles to arctic, there are

This photographs details the variety of equipment and gear carried by a Ranger officer. Dehydrated MRE (Meals Ready to Eat) food packets are in the foreground. A heavy LBE with Motorola radio in the back. Of special interest is the green tape-camouflaged M-16A2. (John Galetzka)

a variety of packing lists. The basic temperate packing list starts with a large waterproof bag, green on the outside and rubbery black on the inside. It is turned inside out and placed inside the ALICE. Turning it inside out prevents static electricity and also prevents reflections from other light sources at night. Most of the gear will be placed within this waterproof bag. The packing list includes an H-harness used to attach the ALICE to a parachute harness for parachute operations. A 15-ft lowering line is used to drop the ALICE and keep it within 15 feet of the jumper. It also protects the paratrooper from possible injury caused by the heavily laden ruck. An ALICE will almost always contain the following: matches, a spare PC, a spare set of BDUs, 550-cord, flashlight, leather gloves for work, black gloves with green inserts, lightweight Gortex top and bottom, lightweight poncho and liner, a shaving kit with a razor and blades, soap in a plastic dish, toothpaste/powder with brush, foot powder, insect repellant ("bug juice"), camouflage stick (green/loam for jungle or white/loam for desert environment), a sewing kit, a sleeping shirt, one sling rope, three snap-links, a brown T-shirt, brown towel, and a weapons cleaning kit. Berets are never carried to the field.

A small clear plastic bag, carried inside the top flap, will include the Ranger Handbook, note pads, pens and pencils, maps and protractor. A length of green tape is wrapped around each pen as an extra supply. Additional 550-cord, as one can never have enough, and a small signaling mirror (also used for shaving), are also included. Some Rangers keep cameras in their bag as well.

A standard tool carried either on the belt or ruck would be a multi-purpose tool or knife. A sleeping pad would be folded into a small square and secured to the frame of the ALICE. All Rangers wear watches and some have small compasses attached to the wristbands.

For the Somalia operation in 1993, Rangers wore the new Ranger Body Armor (RBA) specifically designed for that mission. Personal vests ranged from traditional flak jackets to new and improved third generation Ranger Body Armor. Nonetheless, body armor is usually too cumbersome to be useful in hot climates.

Additional personal equipment includes water hydration systems (a tubular bag with a flexible tube akin to a moldable straw used by the soldier, leaving his hands free) carried on the back, pads for elbows and knees as well as a variety of goggles.

Weapons/Night Optical Devices (NODS)

The Ranger's primary weapon was originally the M-16A1 and then the M-16A2 version, which differs only in that it has a three-round burst capacity instead of the automatic capability of its predecessor. Currently, the 75th Ranger Regiment uses the M-4 carbine with several aiming devices. A shortened variant of the M-16A2, the M-4A1 5.56mm carbine assault rifle is a lightweight, gas-operated, air-cooled, magazine-fed, selective rate, shoulder-fired weapon with a collapsible stock. It is capable of fully automatic fire and features a flat top rail for mounting day/night sights and a detachable carrying handle. It also mounts all accessories common to the M-16A2, including the M-203 40mm grenade launcher. One of the fundamental requirements of the Ranger is to fight at night: as a matter of fact, he prefers it. Various generations of day/night optical devices (NODs) improve his ability to conduct combat operations in the dark. Sights include the Trijicon TA01NSN ACOG 4x32 scope, the PEQ2 Laser System/Infra-Red, M-64, and the AN/TVS-5 crew served weapon sight. A third generation 7-D (NOD) or monocular version is strapped to the new Kevlar helmet – the MICH (Modular/Integrated Communications Helmet), issued in 2002.

A modified M-249 SAW with pistol grip. He wears elbow pads, a new generation of Ranger body armor and carries a water hydration system on the back: the proto-typical urban warrior. (Nancy Fisher, USASOC)

A Ranger in 2002 carrying an M-4 with blank adapter and body armor/load-carrying system. He presses down on an internal microphone in his new helmet to communicate with other squad members. (Justin Viene, 2/75 PAO)

The Squad Automatic Weapon (SAW) is the M-249. The M-60 machine gun, which was capable of heavier automatic fire, was replaced by the superior M-240G in the mid-1990s. Personal sidearms have included the .45-cal and 9mm automatic pistols.

A variety of hand grenades, ranging from concussion to smoke to flash-bang, provide additional offensive and defensive capabilities. Anti-tank/personnel weapons range from the 90mm recoilless rifle, to the Carl Gustav, Javelin, AT-4 and the LAW (Light Antitank Weapon). 60mm

The Carl Gustav anti-armor weapon with aiming device. Note the bracket for night optics attached to the front of the Kevlar helmet. (Nancy Fisher, USASOC)

The Ranger Regiment's Table of Organization and Equipment (TOE) includes motor cycles. In the background is a Ranger Special Operations Vehicle (RSOV). Note flak vests and LBE. (John Galetzka)

mortars and even the 120mm mortars are also found within the Regiment Table of Organization and Equipment.

Each Ranger battalion possesses 12 Ranger Special Operations Vehicles (RSOVs) for airfield seizure missions. The vehicle is a modified Land Rover and carries a crew of six. Normally, each vehicle mounts an M-240G machine gun and either an MK-19 grenade launcher or an M2 .50 cal heavy machine gun. One member of the crew mans an anti-armor weapon. The main purpose of these vehicles is to provide a mobile, defensive capability. Each battalion also possesses ten 250cc motorcycles that assist in providing security and mobility during airfield seizures. In May 2002, new light armored personnel carriers were introduced to the regiment to provide organic armored punching power. Rubber boats, specialty parachute and underwater diving gear complete the Rangers' warfighting capabilities.

Rangers are capable of conducting operations on land, air and sea. Care of equipment is drilled into Rangers constantly. The Ranger haircut, the "high-and-tight," is visible. (John Galetzka)

RANGER BATTALION

I will always endeavor to uphold the prestige, honor,
and "esprit de corps" of my Ranger Battalion.

The new Ranger, fresh from RIP graduation, arrives at the Replacement Depot at Fort Lewis, Washington. All new personnel report to the depot prior to processing in at their new duty station. A few days later the Ranger processes in at the Headquarters Company of the 2nd Battalion, 75th Ranger Regiment. The building is situated on one of the four corners surrounding a large field commonly known as the Quad. The other three companies, A, B and C, complete the quadrangle. Pull-up bars painted gold and black, the colors of the Ranger Tab, line the entrances to each company.

The Ranger reports to the sergeant-major of the battalion. Here he is informed of what he and the battalion expect of one another. A few minutes later he is on his way to his new company where he reports to the First Sergeant, the NCO responsible for the day-to-day operations of his company. He will know more about his Rangers' abilities and problems than any other man at the unit. And he also knows exactly where the new Ranger is needed.

The Scrolled Ranger then makes his way to the chow-hall a few meters away. As he dons his new beret, several trucks pull up and a throng of Rangers pile out and welcome their new comrade. "Get down, you newbie expletive, you tabless bitch," shouts the 20-year-old Ranger School "tabbed" specialist. Push-ups and more push-ups follow – all elevated. And finally, "Recover." The newbie scrambles to his feet and stands at parade-rest in front of a staff sergeant. As luck would have it, this staff sergeant is his new squad leader and a monster of a man who does not like other Rangers messing with his men. He makes this perfectly clear when he comes across the Spec-4 mafia hazing the new Ranger. The "mafia" is a group of specialists who have graduated Ranger School and continue to ensure that all new members of the regiment are motivated and live up to the regiment's high standards.

The Ranger follows his squad leader and his new Ranger buddies up the staircase to the squad room. His new home, shared with three other Rangers, is also the squad's room. As a few Rangers receive promotions, the rooms became less crowded until a double becomes available. One of the tabless or Scrolled Rangers accompanies the new member for the next few days to make sure he gets his gear and uniforms squared away according to regimental standard operating procedures.

Rangers do not need to know the Army Song, but they had better have memorized the *Ranger Creed* and Rogers' *Standing Orders,* the two main staples of Ranger tradition. The *Ranger Creed* was written by Command Sergeant Major Gentry in 1974 and served as a code of conduct for the two newly founded Ranger battalions. The Regiment retained the *Creed* and to this day it represents the core of Ranger philosophy. Rogers' *Standing Orders* proclaim 19 short rules of Ranger-type warfare beginning with the most famous of all its stanzas, "Don't forget nothing." Although these orders are credited to colonial Ranger, Robert Rogers (1731–95), the reality is that they are derivatives of his original 28 *Rules of Discipline.* How the official Rules changed to the

Confident, well trained, and supremely fit, these Rangers wear the battalion black physical training uniform. (John Galetzka)

"Maggots" in Germany in 1987. The Ranger battalions deploy regularly overseas. These maggots carry a 60mm mortar and a 90mm recoilless rifle and consider themselves superior to all other Rangers who carry lighter loads. (Steve Toth)

commonly accepted Standing Orders remains a mystery. Nonetheless, if a Ranger fails to memorize the Creed or the Standing Orders, he will find himself doing a lot of push-ups.

And push-ups are done the Ranger way – elevated. Either near vertical push-ups against the side of the wall, or against the six-foot wall locker in the room or the famous Ranger Rock at the entrance of the company. This rock is a good-sized black painted boulder and has enough surface area to accommodate at least half a dozen Rangers' boots.

At a Ranger battalion, there are line-dogs, maggots and pogues. A "line dog" is a standard Ranger rifleman. A "maggot" is a Ranger that humps (carries) heavier weapons systems such as the machine gun, a mortar or an anti-armor gun. A person working for a headquarters company is a "pogue." Pogues spend very little time rangering, although it is their work that makes the battalion one of the most efficient units in the US Army. The new member of the squad learns these intricacies rather quickly. He does not fraternize with other platoons in general, even during his off-time. His platoon is his world and his squad is his family. He also happens to be assigned to a weapons squad (machine guns).

An average day

It is dark outside. A loud bang startles some Rangers awake, others are already about. One of the CQ (Charge of Quarters) runners bangs his Kevlar helmet against the doors of each room down the hall. This is the wake-up call. Men stumble out of their beds to the latrines. Married Rangers who live off-post roll into the parking lot outside the company. It is about 0530. After quick attention to personal hygiene and some barracks maintenance, namely cleaning the toilets and showers, one of the Rangers checks the company bulletin board for that morning's physical training uniforms and time of first formation – 0630. The uniform is the all-black Ranger T-shirt, running shorts with the 2nd Battalion Ranger scroll and running shoes with white socks.

The new Ranger exits the company building and performs 10 pull-ups, as is customary for non-Ranger School qualified personnel. He then runs to his respective position within the squad. Being the newest member he will be at the end of the squad formation. The platoon sergeants are in front of each platoon. "Tab check," grunts one man after the other. All tabless Rangers complete 25 push-ups, and one for the "Ranger in the Sky" (a mythical God-like figure), another for 2nd Batt, another one for his company, his squad, his team, his gun. Finally, the First Sergeant arrives as shouts of "get squared away" echo throughout the formation. The platoon sergeants call the platoons to attention. Morning reports are taken and eventually the company falls out to conduct physical training.

Today each platoon conducts its own physical training; in this instance a mild warm-up of stretching and calisthenics is followed by an eight-mile run. The Ranger standard for a five-mile run is eight minutes per mile. However, the regimental standard for the Headquarters of the Ranger Regiment at Fort Benning, Georgia, is a little different at Fort Lewis, Washington, the home of the 2nd Ranger Battalion. As the platoon moves out smartly and passes the six-foot chain-link wooden slat fence which separates the battalion from the rest of the post, other regular Army units are performing their runs. One of the Ranger sayings is "Rangers lead the way." And lead the way they do. The new Ranger, along with his platoon, sprints by the other formations. Once well clear of those slower "legs," the pace settles to a comfortable six- or seven-minute mile. Some Rangers fall out because of the fast pace, but Rangers never leave fallen comrades, so the platoon circles back repeatedly to allow the lagging Rangers to link back up prior to returning to the Quad. Some of the Rangers, tabbed and untabbed, will perform remedial runs in the future. The men return to the company area, conduct more physical training as well as a "police call," when Rangers form a line and pick up any garbage near their company. They return to their rooms to take quick showers, eat at the dining facility and get ready for their next formation at 0900 hours. The newbie learns quickly to check the company's bulletin board regularly for the day's training.

The Rangers stand in loose formation outside, awaiting the arrival of the First Sergeant or company commander. They wear "fluffs and buffs," field uniforms and blackened boots. Most of them chew tobacco – one of the trademarks of a Ranger. Large rucks lie in front of their feet with weapons resting against them. No weapon is ever placed on the ground and everything is "dress right dress" – neatly placed according to Ranger operating procedure. Today, they notice Headquarters Company, the pogues, moving out with rucksacks and rifles to conduct their weapons qualification. Whistles, cat-calls and abuse are hurled at them as they pass by the line companies.

Soon the company comes to attention and the First Sergeant hands command to the company commander. The platoon sergeants and First Sergeant move to the rear of the formation as the officers, previously in the

An enlisted man's room used to house at least two Rangers in the 1980s. These rooms are impeccably clean during the week. The multi-colored blanket is an issue item. The 3rd Ranger Battalion's barracks at Fort Benning, Georgia, are more like college dormitories than traditional army barracks. (John Galetzka)

Rangers are extremely competitive and, time permitting, the battalions hold company competitions called "Banner Days." Companies compete against one another in some rather tough games, often leading to numerous injuries. The best company wins a banner that adorns its Company Guidon. (John Galetzka)

back, run to the front on the command of "Post," uttered by the captain. All Ranger officers are senior in their rank. A platoon leader in the regular Army is a 2nd lieutenant with a few months of active duty. In a Ranger battalion he must be a 1st lieutenant with one command under his belt. Only in rare exceptions can a 2nd lieutenant become a platoon leader in the Rangers: he must first have been an enlisted man with service in the Regiment. Company commanders are also second-tour captains. The Ranger officer corps is made up of seasoned leaders. The captain gives a quick pep talk and the companies fall out to conduct their training.

Today's mission is simple – the Ranger squads will force-march to a location and repel an attack. Each mission is based on real world scenarios and is tailored to a specific foreign country. A road march of 12 miles normally takes three hours to complete. Realism is a trademark of Ranger training and realism has reduced the traditional three-man machine gun team to two. The new recruit, at battalion for only a few short months, is the gunner, his buddy, an even newer arrival, is promoted from ammo bearer to assistant gunner, and the two must carry the equipment normally carried by three. Tripod, spare barrel, traverse and elevating device, binoculars, 900 rounds of linked ammunition, a couple of training aids, concrete claymore mines and grenades. And to top it off, the assistant has to carry a rifle for added fire power. Each maggot carries roughly 100lb, including personal gear. There they are in all their Ranger glory – weighed down like a couple of jackasses. Some more seasoned Rangers with nagging injuries pop "Ranger candy" – pain killers for injuries that were never able to heal while at battalion. The Scrolled Ranger realizes that every day is a hard day at a Ranger battalion. If it is not physically grueling, it is a mental challenge to become familiar with the mass of gear and weapons and to learn about Ranger leadership.

The newbie machine gun team is attached to the 1st squad and the line doggies move out at great speed, whipping past a formation of regular grunts who are themselves on a road march. "Are they on a Sunday stroll?" the Rangers think. Soon the line doggies, on a terrific pace, are well ahead of the two-man gun team. And the maggots are annoyed. "Bastards," mutters one, shifting his heavy ruck into a less painful position. Although the ALICE has a belt, Ranger SOP prohibits the use of it, and the burden is placed on the shoulders. The lower pad rests against the kidneys. The gun team falls further behind, the gap with the line doggies widens. The maggots jog to catch up. A couple of yards behind are the First Sergeant and platoon leader, observing and conversing. A few minutes later they catch up, only to realize that the assistant gunner is overheated and woozy. He is humping way too much gear for this pace and the free swinging arm motion, so helpful when road marching, is impeded by his rifle. They slow down and talk briefly. One of the line dogs is called back and the equipment split up.

Rangers in the late 1980s. The ever faithful ALICE forces the Rangers to lean forward to compensate for the weight. (John Galetzka)

A couple of miles later they hit a defensive line and the squad spreads out. The machine gun rests on its bipod legs, the rucks are off and to the side. The assistant links all the ammo into one consecutive link. This is not ideal, as linked ammunition can get twisted and cause a malfunction, and any movement with the gun is impossible with the long ammunition belts. But his actions are influenced by his exhaustion. Targets pop up down the range at various distances and are engaged by the squad. Having been taught the proper firing technique since his first day with the Rangers, the machine gunner knows he must pull the trigger, not squeeze it. A six- to nine-round burst is accomplished by

A classic three-man M-60 machine gun team. On the far left is the armed ammunition bearer, the assistant gunner and at the bottom of the photo, the gunner using the tripod. The gunner is in the classic prone position with cocked right leg. (Author's collection)

thinking, "fire burst of six," while pulling the trigger. The noise is terrific. The firing stops and the squad regroups about a hundred yards to the rear of the range. Kevlar helmets are replaced with patrol caps. As the men field-clean their weapons they hear bits and pieces of a conversation between the First Sergeant and the squad leader. "Your squad was tired and almost incoherent... you moved too fast..." So the line dogs did shoot poorly. The two maggots exchange looks, knowing their performance was also pretty bad, and break out some snacks, waiting to road-march back to the battalion.

By early afternoon the Rangers are back at their company cleaning their weapons in the squad room. Empty soft drink cans are used as spitoons for the spit generated by chewing tobacco. The atmosphere is relaxed, a few Rangers "work" on their push-ups. The gun teams compete against one another by disassembling and assembling the machine guns, sometimes blindfolded. By 1700, all weapons are returned to the armory, and the platoon assembles in the hallway of their floor. The platoon leader gives a weekend safety briefing: "Don't drink if you are underage. Nobody drink and drive. If you need a ride, call somebody to bring you back to base." The platoon is anxious to go and start the weekend. Hard training requires hard partying. The barracks rats, as Rangers who rarely leave the compound are known, are anxious to buy and consume massive amounts of alcohol, all in the safety of their rooms and hallways while others party elsewhere, usually local strip clubs or music clubs in Seattle. Once dismissed, vehicles peel out of the parking lots, some returning shortly with cases of beer. Whether they stay or leave, the soldiers drink and drink and drink. Some drive. And some drink and drive and get caught. They are gone the next day, down the road to one of the despised regular units. A fate worse than death – or so it seems. The partying is fun and a great release for pent-up frustrations. On occasion, fights break out with civilians or "leg" soldiers. By Monday morning the assembled formation reeks of alcohol and more than one Ranger pukes his guts out during the run – but all manage to finish, no matter their condition.

Working off stress is an important release valve for hard training. Like all good Rangers, the platoon not only trains together, but parties together as well. (John Galetzka)

"Hazing" is intended to ensure that "newbies" are motivated and dedicated to being Rangers. A good sense of humor is required. (John Galetzka)

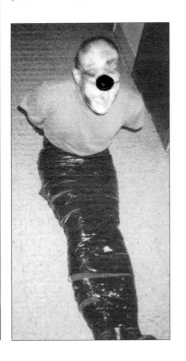

Hazing

Weeknights, away from the prying eyes of Ranger officers and senior NCOs (Non-commissioned officers), the tabless Rangers are low-crawling in sleeping bags up and down the staircases. Others are locked inside six-foot-tall wall lockers before being pushed down the staircase. The "hazing" process is intended to weed out the less-dedicated individuals. In the field, "koalifying" might take place, where a soldier is hung upside down from a telephone pole or tree. Most of the hazing is good-natured, but if a Ranger runs foul of someone in his unit, his time at battalion is tough, and usually ends with him quitting or getting sent to another company.

Memorizing the Ranger Handbook, the bible for all Ranger techniques and tactics, from surviving the harsh elements to calling in air strikes, is an absolute must. Failure to answer questions correctly leads to more smoke sessions. Although a Scrolled Ranger is at the bottom of the totem pole at his unit, he is still a "battboy," a soldier raised in the best infantry unit in the world, the Ranger battalion.

The Ranger has been at battalion for a number of months. He is squared away and his Ranger buddies value him as a member of the squad. The battalion goes on block leave for 14 days. Most Rangers go home for those short weeks to tell stories and revel in the admiration of their peers and families. The young Ranger is no different. He is excited to see his father and family and to discover what his old friends are up to nowadays. Invariably, they are attending college or working, certainly leading less exciting lives than him. More than satisfied, he is anxious to go to Ranger School.

Each Ranger battalion and company has its own identity. "A" company, known as Alpha Company by some, is the home of the "Alphabots." Alphabots are known to be so uptight and overwhelmingly strict that even in the harsh environment of a Ranger battalion, they are mocked and ridiculed by the other companies. The men of Charlie Company, with their slightly longer hair and more loosely maintained barracks, seem to be from a different unit altogether. And Bravo Company, naturally, is the happy medium. Some platoons give themselves nicknames, such as "Earth Pigs" or *Vatos Locos* ("Crazy Boys").

JUMP TRAINING AND COMBAT EXERCISES

Training is relentless and block leave short. Parachuting is one of the most common insertion methods used by the Rangers. To stay jump-certified a Ranger must jump at least once every three months, although they usually jump twice a month, sometimes weekly. Low-level parachute jumps are used for airfield seizures or as a means to rapidly deploy large numbers of soldiers in a short amount of time. Typically, it takes a

Ranger battalion 30 minutes from the time of the jump until fully assembled and ready to move toward their intended target. Parachuting at a Ranger battalion is not the same as jumping at Airborne School. The rucks weigh more, both doors of the aircraft are shot-gunned and almost emptied simultaneously, and finally, the Rangers move fast and furiously once on the ground.

A typical Ranger parachute drop begins with sustained airborne training. The companies assemble at an area in the Quad on wooden bleachers where they listen to a briefing. They have already received mission briefs and are fully aware of the task before them: a night drop into the desert to assault a defensive line in the mountains, for example. Now the jumpmasters detail the drop zone, such as the expected wind conditions and myriad other details, all vital to the successful execution of the parachute assault. Once briefed, the Rangers jog to an area behind their barracks to practice parachute landing fall (PLF) techniques and emergency procedures, including water landings, electrical hazards, hung or intertwined jumpers. Platoon sergeants yell "double-time" to initiate the jog and the formation of Rangers breaks out with the famous airborne cadence of "Airborne, airborne, all the way, airborne, airborne, everyday. We like it here, we love it here, we've finally found a home."

Hours later the Ranger and his company gather in the Quad with rucks and weapons. The manifest is called, and Rangers line up in their positions for final loading. All Rangers cross load, in the event that one of the aircraft is lost either by accident or battle, there will be enough men spread through the various other aircraft to accomplish their missions. Otherwise, one lost aircraft could spell doom on an entire mission objective. Dog tags are checked against the manifest and everything is physically verified. Finally, cattle trucks, large enough and uncomfortable enough to carry cattle, arrive and the Rangers are driven to a nearby airfield where they unload, draw parachutes and begin the process of donning the equipment. Although newer parachutes are used and trained with, the Regiment prefers the T-10, as it limits the mobility of the jumper, thus avoiding midair collisions.

The complete package is cumbersome and precise: one Ranger, parachute on his back, a reserve to his front and directly below it, his upside-down ruck with 15-foot lowering line. A weapons-carrying container, the M-1950, is tied down to his left leg; underneath the parachute harness is his LBE, and finally his Kevlar is on his head. Ranger buddies give each other a cursory once-over as Ranger jumpmasters check their equipment. All Rangers are helped into a prone position where they wait for the signal to load onto the birds. Finally, the Rangers help each other up and they waddle toward the aircraft which seems to be miles away. Under the excruciating weight of their packs, the men can take only tiny steps of 6–12 inches; their backs ache, and it is a matter of pride not to rest as they struggle toward the bird. Once loaded and seated, finally clear of the foul-smelling aircraft fuel, the paratroopers are already tired. There is no room in the C-130. The Ranger cadence of "C-130 rolling down the strip, 64 Rangers on a one-way trip," tells little of the complete lack of space. The Rangers are packed like sardines in a tin can, their knees interlocking with those of the men facing them.

The burden of the nation rests on the back of its warriors. A terrific picture of the enormous amount of gear strapped onto a human being for airborne operations. The tiger stripe camouflage face paint is visible. The paratroopers are dependent on each other to get off the floor. (John Galetzka)

The jumpmasters run across the mass of Rangers, from one end of the aircraft to another. Sometimes the weight of the metal frame of the ALICE will leave a bruise as it digs into someone's thighs. Airsick Rangers throw up into small bags; others pull jokes on the Air Force (AF) personnel, a favorite being to take a bag of beans from the MRE (Meals Ready to Eat) and place them unseen into an airsickness bag. As an AF crewmember comes by one Ranger will hold the bag to his face, pretending to empty his stomach. Another Ranger pulls out his plastic spoon from his still accessible chest pocket and begins to eat the delicacy. The desired effect is achieved as the victim turns in disgust.

The Army Rangers are belted in and have fallen asleep as the aircraft taxies for take-off. Sometime later, they are nudged awake – it is time to jump. They briefly check their equipment for a final time. The smell of vomit and stale air is almost too much to bear, but once the doors whip open and the noise level intensifies, the fresh cold air is wonderful and the young Ranger truly loves it. The signals for the jump procedure stir the Rangers into action. "Six minutes," yell the jumpmasters, one on each door. The commands are repeated loudly by all Rangers, including hand and arm signals for each command. Pointing with both hands to the exterior row of Rangers: "All outboard personnel, stand up." The Rangers closest to the skin of the bird are lifted up by the men facing them. The hand and arm motion is repeated, followed by "All inboard personnel, stand up." The interior two rows of Rangers struggle up. "Hook up." The static line, the yellow cord responsible for pulling the main chute out of the bag, is attached to a central cable running the length of the aircraft and a safety pin is pushed through and bent over. "Check equipment." The Rangers quickly check each other's equipment. "Sound off with equipment check." A slap on the butt from the last Ranger in the rear of the bird starts a chain. "OK," is passed along with each slap. In the event of a problem, the Ranger places his free arm over the center cable and a jumpmaster would come and quickly fix the problem or detach the jumper

Although these Rangers are not rigged with parachutes, this picture shows the tight space in an aircraft. C-130s, 141s and 17s are used for parachute operations. (John Galetzka)

and make him sit down on the aluminum bench to clear the path for the Rangers behind. In this case, no problems are found, and the young Ranger, closest to the exit, points his free arm at the Jumpmaster and simultaneously shouts, "All okay jumpmaster." By now, the one-minute warning has passed. The jumpmasters spend this last minute leaning in and out of the aircraft doors, searching for the drop zone. "Thirty seconds." The interior green light comes on, but the lead Ranger waits for the jumpmaster's okay. Finally it comes, and out he goes.

Gone are the loud roars of the engine and the shouting. It is completely silent as the Ranger hangs upside down, conducting the silent four-second count procedure, "one-thousand, two-thousand..." waiting for the chute to deploy properly. And it does! Whipped back into an upright position, he gently descends toward the Earth, all in total silence and complete darkness. Within a few short seconds he pulls his two nylon straps to release the rucksack, and when he feels a short tug he knows it has reached the end of the 15-foot rope. It hits, he hits. The perfectly practiced five-point landing in reality turns out to have missed one or two parts. Good thing he wore his helmet. And good thing he missed some large boulders just a few feet away. One of the other Rangers slams into one. Although in obvious distress, he is able to remain silent – noise discipline at its finest. The company medic hustles over to attend to his injuries.

It is dark, but the Ranger can make out the rest of his group dropping from the sky as he frees himself from his gear. He dumps the parachute harness and parachute with reserve into an aviator's kit bag. The machine gun, freed from the protective carrier, is locked and loaded with a 100-round belt. The comforting but hateful ALICE is on his back as he throws the heavy aviator bag over his ruck and moves to an area where he drops off his parachute equipment, a practice done only during training exercises. In a combat jump, Rangers concern themselves only with getting into the action. Freed of the exceptional weight, he and several others from his platoon link up and move out. They reach the patrol base after a long hump, drop their rucks and form a perimeter while the leaders conduct a reconnaissance on the target. Time passes slowly in the silence of the desert. In a few short months they would conduct winter or jungle training, but today it is the cold night of the desert, which surely will become blisteringly hot during the day.

As he waits, the Ranger ponders life at the battalion. The rest of the army sleeps, while the Rangers work. He thinks back to a party a few weeks ago, when in a spontaneous ceremony after a few drinks, the Rangers got on their knees and prayed for war. All other professions can practice and apply their training, but the military can only train until a war erupts. The young Ranger remembers his buddy who was dismissed from the unit. The military term for his offense was "fraternizing," which he did with another Ranger's wife. The battalion can be ruthless, exacting and unforgiving. And families play an important part in battalion life. His buddy was sent down to leg land, and they would probably never see each other again.

A T-10 parachute with risers used for minor mobility. This Ranger took enough time to get a snapshot within moments of jumping out of the airplane. (John Galetzka)

Finally, the combat patrol in the desert begins. The mission is to assault a defensive line wired with concertina. Machine guns are posted from nearby hilltops to provide covering fire. It is still dark as they set into their positions. Moments later an aircraft, probably a Warthog, an A-10 tank buster, screams by and hits the enemy lines. The machine gun squad hears and sees mortar rounds pummel the area. Below, tiny blue lights move forward – the small chemical lights attached to the rear of the Rangers' Kevlar helmets. The three machine guns open up in alternating bursts of fire. It sounds like a beautifully choreographed musical. The Ranger sees tracer rounds hitting their intended targets, barely ahead of the advancing Rangers. In spite of all the noise, his weapons squad, on top of a hill, clearly hears a maggot screaming "90" followed by an incredible "BLAM!" Hundreds of flechette rounds, tiny metal arrows, are discharged toward the enemy as another signal indicates that the machine guns should shift fire ahead of the advancing Rangers and well past the defensive lines. The line dogs go in for the kill. A cacophony of

Invasion of Grenada, 1983

1

4

3

2

A

RANGER RGT

1ST RANGER BN

2D RANGER BN

3D RANGER BN

Ranger, B/Co., 3/75, Panama, 1989

B

Ranger, Bravo Company, 3/75, Operation Desert Storm, 1991

C

Ranger, Afghanistan, 2002

Indoctrination, 1980s

1

2

3

E

F

Assault on Rio Hato, Panama, December 1989

G

Mogadishu, October 1993

H

whooping, rebel yells and generic screams intermixes with hand grenades exploding and more small arms fire. It is a beautiful sight to behold. Rangers! Hooah! Shouts of "Cease fire!" and whistles blowing abruptly end the firing. Minutes go by, then a muffled explosion from one of the bunkers. The attack continues a few moments later.

Hours later, weapons squad hears that one of the line doggies had forgotten to disengage the safety on his hand grenade. Once a safe amount of time had elapsed, the team leader of the guilty party went into the bunker, located the grenade and took it out for detonation. Undoubtedly, the guilty Ranger will be reminded of this incident again and again.

A few days later, buses drop the battalion off at Fort Lewis and the company refits. The rest of this day as well as the next are used for refitting damaged equipment and uniforms. It is not uncommon to break the metal frame of an ALICE or to get uniforms so worn that they have to be replaced. Weapons need to be meticulously cleaned and any malfunctions or problems are brought to the attention of the armorer.

It was a great deployment. Morale is high, and the Rangers are looking forward to their well-deserved weekend. Friday afternoon rolls around and Rangers take off for the weekend. They check the company board, making sure that their pager numbers are listed. The battalion has been on RRF1 for the past few weeks, which means the company has to be at full strength within four hours of notification. Failure to be back on time for any Ranger results in dismissal. Civilian food is especially good after a week of the Army's mess and the nightclubs are lively. No one's pager has gone off but our Ranger decides to call the company and see if anything is going on. "Nada, dude" comes the swift reply from the CQ. This process repeats itself a hundred times during the weekend.

Close-quarter battle

Nothing has changed by Monday morning's formation except for the fresh haircuts. The routine continues – physical training, some Rangers combat hangovers, and later on, the company embarks to the Tire House for close-quarter battle training.

The Tire House is exactly that. About eight feet high, it is made entirely of rubber tires filled with sand or concrete and divided into several rooms. A Ranger staple is building entry and clearing techniques. Various methods are taught, and today one can find many variations on the same theme of covering an area. A four-man team stacks up at the door entry with one man pulling rear security. What looks like a simple toss of a grenade through a door is actually done with great care. The grenade-lobbing individual must look into the room as he throws it, ensuring accuracy in its delivery, otherwise the hard body of the grenade might bounce off the rubber tires and around the room. And that is exactly what happens next. A young Ranger hurls the grenade without

Rangers and wives or girlfriends at the Ranger Ball, a ceremony celebrating the Ranger regiment. It is a formal affair and encourages a closer bond or affiliation to the 75th Ranger Regiment. (John Galetzka)

looking and it bounces off the wall, straight back to the Ranger team. A seasoned Ranger NCO, observing the training, nonchalantly kicks the grenade back into the room and takes one step back for cover behind a wall. The grenade explodes, everything is destroyed, and the team successfully clears the room. Rangers are not a surgical unit: their mission is primarily one of destruction.

The after-action report is another standard practice. After each exercise or training mission, while the events are fresh in their minds, the men assemble and discuss their points of view on the operation. This practice is an invaluable learning tool.

The Ranger has been at battalion for nearly a year now and he has noticed certain changes. Lean and mean Rangers are out, as patrolling through jungles and "dinosaur country" (heavily wooded areas that no one has roamed through other than dinosaurs and Rangers) has fallen out of favor. Beefier, bulkier Rangers who kick in doors and practice city fighting have taken their place. New equipment and men constantly flow into the Ranger Regiment. Advances in night vision devices have made night-fighting a slightly different concept than in previous years. Whereas only a few Ranger leaders would have had NODs in the past, every Ranger now practices with them constantly. Communication equipment also allows more efficient contact between squad members. Emphasis is less on infantry training and more on special operations. Airfield seizures are still a core activity, but a growing number of missions are geared toward supporting Delta Force.

A Ranger battalion deploys to Fort Bragg, North Carolina to conduct special ops missions. In this case, Delta operators travel on small helicopters commonly called "Little Birds," while Rangers fast rope from Black Hawk helicopters at various locations through-out the mock city. The Rangers' mission is to provide security and additional firepower to the Delta elements as they in turn methodically clear rooms and snatch personnel.

Fast roping sounds like fun and looks easy, but it is neither. A normal fast rope takes only a short time to deploy soldiers. The Ranger grabs onto the nylon rope with his gloved hands and basically slides down until he makes contact with the ground, then rapidly moves to his position as other Rangers continue to slide down. There is frequently some kind of dog pile at the bottom of the rope as several Rangers land on top of each other. Nonetheless, Rangers usually land on the ground and roll away, as more often than not the added weight of body armor and machine guns makes for an uncontrolled collision with the ground. Rangers assume good positions and cover their sector while buildings are taken out by Delta. Many of the freshmen Rangers keep looking at the action instead of their own areas of responsibility. This will be discussed in the after-action report later.

During his time at the Ranger battalion, the Ranger has seen many changes at the unit.

For a short time the Ranger regiment adopted the regular army's gray physical training (PT) uniform, another blow to the morale of the unit whose members are driven by the desire to be elite. (John Galetzka)

Some are good, but efforts by the "brass" to streamline the Army, thus making the Rangers less elite, have had a negative impact on morale. The famous black PT uniforms have given way to the Army grays that regular units wear. Distinctive uniforms have been replaced with the regular BDUs, derogatorily called "duckhunters." Rolling or crushing the patrol caps Ranger-style has been prohibited. Posters have come off the walls and a new moral code of conduct has taken over. Whereas in earlier times punishments

were harsh, they were usually just. More frequently, Rangers complain about the ever-present "Big Brother" dominating their lives. Many old hands quit, as well as new Rangers. Seasoned NCOs find themselves micro-managed by worried bosses. But who can blame the bosses at regiment? Too many elite units from different branches are competing for the same dollars. Budgets over time have expanded and shrunk. Having a military career with promotions means not rocking the boat. The Ranger Regiment is still prestigious and a great unit, but the undeniable fact is that turn rates are exceptionally high, many finding the Ranger life too challenging.

Along with these growing pains, there continues to be a problem with some Rangers using drugs, mainly steroids. Drug testing was and is common. A number of Rangers, both enlisted and commissioned, have been "dx'd" (discharged) for using LSD or cocaine.

But the Regiment lives on, Rangers come and go, and finally, after patiently waiting his turn, the Ranger is off to Ranger School. He has waited about a year and he is ready.

Rangers fast roping from Black Hawk helicopters onto the rooftops of a mock city. One problem with fast roping is that in dry terrain the rotor wash will kick up tremendous amounts of dirt causing "brown-outs." (Nancy Fisher, USASOC)

PRE-RANGER AND RANGER SCHOOL

All members of the 75th Ranger Regiment are given the opportunity to attend Ranger School. Ranger School was developed in the 1950s and although the term Ranger is used, the primary purpose of the school is to teach leadership skills. The course is 58 days long and is currently composed of three phases that have evolved over the years.

The 75th Ranger Regiment has created a three-week long "pre-Ranger" course to prepare "Battboys" for the rigors of Ranger School. For most, it serves as a refresher course with familiar, albeit tough material; for others it is a program necessary to fill in any gaps that may exist. Combat and reconnaissance patrols are conducted over and over, until the Ranger is well familiar with the drill. In particular, the pre-Ranger course covers ropes and knots, land navigation and long movements. Factoring in these three weeks, Ranger School for the Scrolled Ranger lasts much longer.

The Benning Phase

The Benning Phase has two parts. The first is conducted at Camp Rogers and includes a physical fitness test where the candidate must complete 49 push-ups, 59 sit-ups, and a two-mile run which must be completed in running shoes within 15:12 minutes or less. Also to be completed are six chin-ups (palms facing toward the face), a combat water survival test, a 5-mile run, several 3-mile runs with an obstacle course, a 16-mile foot march, night and day land navigation tests, medical considerations class, rifle bayonet, pugil stick and combatives (hand-to-hand) exercises. Terrain association, demolitions, patrol base/ORP (Objective Rally Point – a location used for last minute procedure prior to the actual attack or mission), and an airborne refresher jump at Fryar Drop Zone complete this phase.

The second part is conducted at nearby Camp William O. Darby. At Camp Darby the emphasis is on squad combat patrol operations. The Ranger must complete the Darby Queens Obstacle Course and learn the fundamentals of patrolling, the warning order/operations order format and communications. The fundamental skills of combat patrol operations include battle drills, ambush and reconnaissance patrols, enter/clearing a room, airborne and air assault operations. The Ranger student must then demonstrate his expertise through a series of cadre and student-led tactical patrol operations. Following the Benning Phase, students are transported to Camp Frank D. Merrill in Dahlonega, Georgia for the next step.

The Mountain Phase

During the Mountain Phase, students are instructed in military mountaineering tasks as well as techniques for employing a squad and platoon for continuous combat patrol operations within a mountainous environment. They further develop their ability to command and

Class 7 – (19) 76. Ranger School is open to other services and foreign allies. The United States Marine Corps regularly sends personnel to the program. (James Dever, USMC)

control a platoon-size patrol through planning, preparing, and executing a variety of combat patrol missions. The Ranger student receives five days of training on military mountaineering where he learns about knots, belays, anchor points, rope management and the basic fundamentals of climbing and rappelling.

At the conclusion of the Mountain Phase, the non-airborne qualified personnel are taken by bus to the final phase of Ranger training, conducted at Camp Rudder, Florida. The airborne-qualified Rangers take a faster route, parachuting in from military transport.

The Florida Phase

The objective of this phase is to sharpen the Ranger student's combat arms functional skills. He must be capable of operating effectively under conditions of extreme mental and physical stress. This is accomplished through practical exercises in extended platoon-level patrol operations in a jungle/swamp environment.

Technique training includes: small boat operations, ship-to-shore operations, expedient stream-crossing techniques, and skills needed to survive and operate in a jungle/swamp environment. Upon completion of the Florida Phase of training, students conduct an airborne insertion into Fort Benning.

The distinct phases of Ranger School will stay with an individual forever, although few will be able to recall the daily events with clarity. Little sleep and even less food grind the Ranger student down over the subsequent eight weeks. Respite is given only a few hours at a time during the course. The rest of the time is spent patrolling, and at some point the Ranger must lead his unit through a patrol. Fulfilling the role of platoon leader and motivating teammates to accomplish the mission can be extremely trying and end in utter failure. The young Ranger receives criticism from the cadre as some members of his patrol were found asleep during an ambush, and their volume of fire was too low.

As the days pass, the Ranger is further worn down from lack of sleep and food. Rangers have died during training at the battalions and during Ranger School, with mental and physical fatigue often a factor. Our Ranger keeps his resolve as he thinks about his father constantly. Knowing failure is not an option, he is determined to return to his unit with the tab. He knows if he does fail, he will be recycled into the next class and given an opportunity to complete the phase, but all this misery and hard work would have been for nothing. Our Ranger is lucky in that his squad is made up entirely of "Battboys" and they get along fairly well, having a common background and goal. Unfortunately for the "Battboys," the rest of the class has a number of "outsiders," soldiers from other units, branches of the military, or even foreign armies.

One unique aspect of Ranger School is that the squad can "peer" individuals. This process allows for a squad to eliminate some members who may not be pulling their weight or who steal food, a common occurrence. The squad does peer two officers. At other times the "Battboys" may fall victim to peering when a squad is made up of non-Rangers. A number of individuals quit or recycle because of an injury or inability to perform to the required standard. They will try again when another class comes through this particular phase of training. Finally, the

Class 11 – 89. A noticeable difference is the size of Ranger classes. Ranger School is not always voluntary – today, all infantry officers are required to attend the school. (Author's collection)

end is near, and the Ranger knows that short of a catastrophe he will graduate. Although exhausted, life is now far less stressful. The surviving group fun-jumps into Fort Benning and finally, graduates from Ranger School. The black and gold tab is pinned onto their shoulders. Four hundred soldiers had begun the course and only 200 made it to graduation. It is worth mentioning that 99 percent of all Battalion Rangers graduate the course.

A few days later, the Ranger is back at the Quad, and a new rotation of personnel cycling in and out at battalion is under way. Attrition rates are high, with up to 60 percent rotating annually, either quitting or being dropped. At the end of their three to four-year enlistments, some Rangers re-enlist for an additional two to four years, while others join Special Forces or Delta, but most leave the service altogether. Disillusionment with the lifestyle and the frustration of constantly training and preparing for an elusive war are frequently cited. Some are simply ready to begin their civilian lives, having served their country. However, life goes on and it is the newly tabbed Ranger's turn to call a tab check (where all non-Ranger School qualified personnel would do push-ups). He has two and a half years left in his enlistment. The battalion lives on.

Specialty Schools
Once tabbed, a Ranger can attend several military courses. These include free-fall parachuting courses such as HAHO (High Altitude, High Opening) or HALO (High Altitude, Low Opening) or possibly water operations related schools such as SCUBA (Self Contained Underwater Breathing Apparatus) or Scout Swimmer. He may also attend the Army Sniper School.

EXPERIENCE OF BATTLE

Energetically will I meet the enemies of my country.
I will never leave a fallen comrade.

Fighting in the jungles – Grenada and Panama

On October 25, 1983, elements of the 1st and 2nd Ranger Battalions conducted a low-level parachute assault onto the Point Salinas airfield in Grenada. Briefings indicated the weather conditions to be good and resistance minimal, if any. Rangers were sprawled on the airfield, some loading aircraft, others still waiting to get a bird. As it turned out, there were not enough aircraft available and a number of Rangers were left behind. It was an ugly sight to behold. With vocal frustration, some Rangers would quit the battalion and others who had thought of extending their original enlistment would not. They had trained hard and the opportunity to put all that training to good use was wasted because of a lack of aircraft.

The Rangers were rigged and ready for a parachute assault when word was passed that the tarmac of Point Salinas was clear of debris and they would air-land instead. The men derigged their equipment only to be told 20 minutes prior to arrival that indeed they would conduct a parachute assault. The Rangers re-equipped themselves without final jumpmaster checks and some individuals did not have time to rerig their heavy rucks. Some of these individuals tucked claymore mines and M-60 ammunition into the front of their jungle fatigues.

As the C-130s battled their way through thunderstorms and finally approached Point Salinas, searchlights and heavy antiaircraft fire greeted them. Some aircraft dropped their jumpers through heavy flak, but most of the follow-on birds pulled away, waiting for the AC-130 Spectre gunship to destroy the antiaircraft weapons systems. The rest of the Rangers dropped after that. Ranger Allen described the scene this way:

With the delays in the jump, we ended up conducting a daylight combat assault instead of the night drop we had planned for. When we landed on the runway I derigged my parachute and started to move with some other Rangers to the platoon assembly area. While we were moving, we began receiving small arms fire from the surrounding hillsides. While a group of us cleared debris from the runway [for follow-on forces to airland], others provided suppressive fire. After I reached the assembly area I linked up with my mortar section and waited for the rest of the mortar gun crews to assemble. Once we had all the section [squad] assembled, we laid in our mortars to fire in direct support of our company. I saw two bulldozers about 200 meters north of our position, so I took two other Rangers with me as security and moved to the bulldozers. We checked them for booby-traps and then started them because the keys were still in the ignitions. We drove to our position and built dirt parapets around each mortar position. At about 1800 hours a company from the 82nd Airborne moved into our sector and relieved us.

A Ranger School graduate with black and gold tab freshly pinned onto the shoulder. Note the Ranger "crush" in the patrol cap. (Arvid Straume)

Panama

The 2nd and 3rd (-) Ranger Battalions conducted a parachute assault onto the airfield at Rio Hato to neutralize 6th and 7th Rifle Companies of the Panamanian Defense Force (PDF). Although Rangers practice airfield seizures regularly, it is interesting to note the confusion and time delays encountered by the Rangers on the ground. Furthermore, although realistic training is a vital part of preparing for war, it does not accurately represent the experiences of the men on the ground. A Ranger sergeant from the 2nd Battalion describes in honest detail the emotional aspect of Rangers at war:

> Our morale was pretty low prior to our deployment to Panama for Operation Just Cause, I know mine was. Switching from the OG 107s to the leg BDUs and giving up the black PT sweats for the regular Army gray ones were just part of the overall mess. Our Battalion Commander (BC) and Sergeant-Major certainly did not make things any better.
>
> I remember drawing my ammo based on position-specific cards. So if you were a machine-gunner, you'd get a card with a specific load for your weapon and my ruck weighed a ton. Anyhow, I was in the bird with the BC and had about 15 guys in front of me. The thing that was interesting was that a number of Rangers were pulled off the birds to make room for the BC's security element, basically cooks with sniper rifles, instead of having front-line troops. And to top that one, one line-doggie had to make room for an officer from the Regiment. I could only shake my head at that.
>
> The chalk was cross-loaded but my whole squad was on board. We all wore the "Bob Marley" camouflage on our Kevlars to help identify the bad guys who did not have them. We expected stiff resistance from at least one rifle and one mechanized company at Rio Hato of around 400 or so Panamanians. Our expected assembly time was 30 minutes – it turned out to be 90 minutes. I was the eleventh at my AA [assembly area] after 60 minutes. We also expected a 2,000lb bomb to lay waste on one of our objectives.
>
> The C-130 had interior red lights and I heard someone reciting the Ranger Creed and all I could think was what a cheese-eating bastard that guy was. Once I jumped, I looked over my shoulder for the enemy barracks which should have been on fire or destroyed by the 2000lb bomb, but nothing. I did not see tracers, too busy looking for damage I suppose. It felt more like a training jump then a combat one. I felt religious. When I realized the barracks were still there I thought the plan had gone awry, after all they (Intel) had told us that we

Two Rangers in an RSOV in Panama during the days of the invasion. The LBE is hooked onto the roll bar. An M-60 is manned by the passenger and a piece of tape is visible on the stock of the M-16A2, indicating the company of this particular battalion. (Richard Hecht)

should expect these elite Panamanians to fight. I have all these thoughts and nothing seems in proper order so bear with me. I remember being in tent city, drawing my ammo, thinking which one of these [expletive] is gonna die? Maybe me? I thought we'd get massacred. I attempted at that time to prepare myself mentally for the upcoming nightmare.

I was glad to jump, to get off the plane, to stop thinking about fear and then of nothing at all and finally that I know my shit. The funny thing is that you become super-paranoid, you thought the Panamanians could see you in particular, just waiting for you. Nothing prepares you for war.

In retrospect I think that if they had dropped the bomb on the barracks, Lear would not have gotten killed. It pisses me off to this day.

While I was on the plane I was thinking about being a Christian, about killing another human being. Once on the ground a sense of self-preservation took over, and I knew I could do it, no animosity to the Panamanians – just doing my job.

My ruck weighed about 100lb, including 20lb of C-4, and my chute had twisted when it jarred open. I was pissed as this made my descent faster, and I had very little time to untwist the chute [this is done through a combination of bicycling motions with the legs and pushing apart the risers above your head]. Only armchair quarterbacks would make you jump with an M1950 (weapons carrying case). I was worried about getting to my weapon, but once I was on the ground there were lots of other things to worry about. I landed in elephant grass somewhere and something strange happened. I just laid on the ground for about 30 seconds. I didn't even move to get my weapon. The tracers overhead were quite exciting. The grass was high but I could still see yellow lights on vehicles that reminded me of the street sweepers back home. I yanked open one of the two LAWs I had on me as I heard Spectre (AC-130) hit the APC (armored personnel carrier) which ended up crashing into a ditch. I threw my LAW away for some reason and moved on.

I hooked up with Lear who was getting out of his [gear]. I called to him and he pulled out his gun and said 'Is that you Sgt [Deleted]?' I said 'No, it's the Panamanians, and they know my name.' The two of us moved down the runway as other Rangers were moving toward their AAs. We encountered an E-6 (Staff Sergeant) who was yelling the running password at us and then waited for a countersign. I told him that it was a running password and that he was a [expletive].

To the west I noticed some anti-aircraft fire at ground level. Why was it firing that low? I turned around and there were about 40 or so Rangers from C/Co, 2/75 behind us.

Trucks were parked across the runways, obviously intended to prevent us from air-landing.

I hooked up with Sgt [deleted] and mortars [section] and followed a path of chemlights to our AA (I found out later that the chemlights were laid out by our platoon leader). I wasn't sure if it was a good thing, the PDF could follow those lights as well. I

An excellent photograph of Rangers from Bravo Company, 2/75, hours after the successful combat parachute assault at Rio Hato, Panama, 1989. These men earned the "mustard stain," a gold star in the middle of the airborne wings indicating a combat jump. Note the knee pads used by some Rangers during airfield seizures. (Rodney LeMay)

thought everyone had already moved out and that I would be dx'd (discharged), but like I said earlier I was the eleventh Ranger there. So we waited and checked our equipment repeatedly.

AA to Objective 1

After about 90 minutes from the drop we moved out. Third squad was in the lead, breaching fences, and clearing buildings, we leap-frogged by squads. The 40mm HE round needs some yards to arm, so we had a few duds. To the south of the objective there was some kind of NCO-type club building. On the left was a latrine or some sort of shack. I threw a stun grenade to clear the building – nothing. SSG [deleted] yelled: 'Are you sure you threw a grenade?' Well, what can you do – I was pissed.

At Objective 1 there was no sign of the enemy. We were led to believe that over 400 elite Panamanians would be here. Now I was really pissed because they had scared the [expletive] out of me earlier. Well, we established a defensive perimeter.

Objective 1 to Objective 2

My squad took the lead. I was wearing NODs which give a hazy green view. At this time, I was concerned that we may have bypassed the PDF [Panama Defense Force]. Maybe they're behind us? I fell down a 20–30-foot ravine with another Ranger, a PFC (Private First Class). I told Lear to continue on until I could get the two of us out of the hole. Malecha, Jr. pulled us out while the other squads (1st Platoon) moved forward.

We caught up to the platoon a little while later in a tree line. I called out to a Ranger from another platoon who was part of the aid and litter teams. He did not respond to my calls. Finally I walked over and kicked him in the head. He responded finally, he was an E-6.

Rangers were screaming for people to get down. Six feet away I saw SSG [deleted] on the ground, shot through the chest, and Lear dead. It didn't really hit me right away but then – damn, tunnel vision, this can't be happening...

We continued to clear buildings via stairs, fired over walls, tossed grenades and so on. I saw a Kevlar helmet on fire on the west side of a building. Training does not prepare you for such destruction. Somebody lived here, it could have been our barracks.

The next day I received Lear's M-203 vest and Kevlar. They were full of dried thick syrupy stuff, blood, his blood. It is hard to know what to feel. Was I a good leader? Had I not fallen into that ravine... The squad started to look awfully young to me.

Eventually the 7th ID came to replace us — they were all [expletive] up and I won't forget the BC (Battalion Commander), with a cocked-back Kevlar, driving in an air-conditioned car, yelling at Rangers to buckle their LBEs. Maybe it was time to get out...

Fighting in built-up areas - Somalia

Rangers practice MOUT (Military Operations in Urban Terrain) regularly and have provided Delta Force with a security force since 1980. However, as city fighting has become a more common occurrence throughout the world, the Ranger Regiment has built more of this specialized training into its schedule. In Somalia, Rangers were called into action and realized that a light infantry battalion requires armored support when fighting in urban terrain. An over-reliance on airpower hurt their ability to break loose the surrounded soldiers of these special operations forces. Additionally, Rangers operate at night, and they do so better than any other infantry unit in the world. Daylight raids are a recipe for disaster and should be avoided.

Ranger John Collett recalls in simple and powerful prose the experiences of the Rangers' desperate fight to save the lives of downed crewmen in the heartland of the enemy in Somalia.

It started out as every Sunday had in the four weeks since we arrived in the Mog [Mogadishu, Somalia, Africa]. We woke up when we wanted. There was no first call on Sundays. Everyone was playing volleyball and tanning as usual. All in all, we hadn't hit the ground on a mission for about two weeks. Then word came that we were getting orders to go on a mission. It was October 3, 1993. It didn't occur to anyone until later that the 3rd Ranger Battalion had been formed nine years earlier on this same day.

We got our equipment on as usual, putting on our bullet-proof vests, LCE, K-pot (Kevlar). I carried an M-249 SAW (Squad Automatic Weapon). This was a day-mission so no night vision devices were taken. I had 950 rounds of 5.56mm ammunition and one frag (grenade). We moved to the aircraft which was already spun up. As usual the Little Birds (helicopters) took off first. The Hardy Boys (Delta Force) gave us the thumbs up as they usually did when they flew by. When the bird takes off is when the adrenaline starts pumping. We had two "brown-outs" where we could see nothing, but the pilot held tight and got us right on target. Tin was blowing off the roofs of buildings; people were getting blown around below us. We got the signal to ready the fast rope. I looked at Sgt Ramaglia and we were both making the Catholic cross at the same time. This was our 7th mission and the first time I made the sign of the cross. It felt different this time. As we hovered over the Somalis, waiting to fast rope down, they were waving to us to come down and play, so we did. I hit the ground, got up against a building and started pulling security

Rangers of Bravo Company, 3/75, in Mogadishu, Somalia, two days prior to the 7th mission. Although often considered a failure, the daylight raid was successful in its purpose of capturing numerous key personnel. The Ranger Body Armor (RBA) was specifically manufactured for the Rangers participating in Operation Gothic Serpent. Ranger Berendsen is on the left and Ranger Collett on the far right. (Anton Berendsen)

up the street. There was sporadic gunfire all around us. We ID'd [identified] our target building, then RPGs (rocket propelled grenades) started going off. I saw one of the birds smoking so I knew it had been hit. PFC Errico and SPC (Specialist) DeJesus were engaging targets down the alley, also saying there were people in the trees and the building windows shooting at us.

The Humvees pulled up about then and Sergeant Strucker got out and started talking to Sergeant First Class Watson. The .50-cal on top of the Humvee started hosing (killing) people that were shooting at us. It's funny that at that time I thought to myself, 'Shit – another mission I won't get to fire my SAW.' I could have never been more wrong. We got word that in fact a bird (helicopter) had gone down about two blocks away and that we were going to have to secure it. The Humvees moved out [to take an injured Ranger back to base]. As we were moving, the fire from the enemy increased. Branches were falling from the trees as gunfire hit them. Bullets have a very distinctive sound when they are being shot at you, and not away from you. As we were proceeding up the previous alley, SFC Watson was on the left side of the street and I was on the right. Bullets were hitting above our heads as we were moving out at a trot. He looked over at me, as casual as can be, and said, 'This sucks.'

We were taking fire from the building from people sticking AK-47s and older weapons around the corner and spraying them in our general direction. I yelled at Sergeant Ramaglia to put a 40mm round (M-203) in the alley. He fired a round and it was short, blowing up about 10 meters in front of our position. I told him it was short. He fired a second round and it hit square into the building, blowing it up. We didn't receive near as much effective fire from that corner after that.

SFC Watson knew we were taking a hell of a crossfire, so he pulled PFC Neathery back and put him in the middle of the road behind a rock, a position I would soon occupy for many hours. They threw a frag at us. I looked up and saw it coming through the trees. I saw the spoon hit the ground. It landed about 15 m in

A battle-scarred Humvee (High Mobility Multipurpose Wheeled Vehicle). This photo was taken just hours after the battle. (Anton Berendsen)

front of our position and exploded. PFC Errico yelled 'Frag.' We hit the ground as it exploded. Doe caught some shrapnel in the leg. Errico caught some in the ankle. SFC Watson told us to start pulling back so we could defend until night.

We laid down suppressive fire and a Ranger shot a 'Sammy' (Somali) in the face. A few seconds later he got shot in the right arm and yelled, 'I'm hit.' I was in the prone position at that time in the middle of the road behind some rocks and a mound of dirt. In this position it was hard for the 'Sammys' to effectively engage me. I had a great field of fire. I looked back to watch some Rangers and Delta move up the street we were on. Just as I looked back at them one of the D-boys got shot in the head. It rocked his head back and blood went everywhere. The man behind him grabbed him and started pulling him back to cover. He got shot in the neck. When he got shot he put his hands to his face and screamed. I thought, 'Shit.' I knew the shit had hit the fan.

A Ranger asked SFC Watson for some frags. SFC Watson, in his irritated voice, said: 'Use the LAW on your back.' The Ranger looked back, puzzled, 'The LAW, mother[expletive].' He smiled and pulled the LAW off his back, extended it and fired.

A few minutes later a 'Sammy' walked in front of our position, all chilled out, like nothing was going on. He looked at me and our other positions. I guess he was a recon man, well he didn't get to tell much. Someone behind him yelled something, as the 'Sammy' turned I saw an AK-47 under his shirt. The recon was over. I laid a good burst at him and at the same instant PFC Floyd opened up. The 'Sammy' staggered and fell behind a building. A few minutes later though, a grenade landed about 2 meters in front of me. I thought, 'Oh shit', and put my head behind a K-pot sized rock in from of me. I remember thinking, 'This is it.' The grenade blew up and knocked me around a bit. I looked up and Specialist Kurth was yelling at me. I couldn't understand what he was saying. I looked over and gave SFC Watson the thumbs up. I was happy that I was still alive. [Shortly thereafter] a Sammy came out of a corridor with an RPG and Floyd and I lit him up. He was gone with a puff of smoke. I guess an RPG exploded when we shot him.

Ammo conservation was a big thing. SFC Watson kept reminding us to keep controlled bursts, which we did. We stayed in this position until dark. When it got dark, we started withdrawing to the buildings behind me where we would set up our defenses for the night. We marked our position with an IR strobe, placing it on the roof of the building we were in. This was done so the Little Birds (helicopters) could start doing their gun runs. I've never felt so much relief as when they started lighting up the buildings around us with 7.62 mini guns and 2 1/2 inch rockets. The decision was made that we would stay here until the reaction forces could get us out.

Several hours later it was decided that we needed to move to the next building. Before making the move, a Black Hawk came in and made an IV and ammo resupply [drop]. [During the short time the bird was hovering, it was] blazing away with the mini guns. They were taking all kinds of fire. Any time a bird came into the area the enemy fire would pick up.

Classic pose of two M-203 grenadiers in Somalia. Note the two distinct patterns of the desert uniforms. The 203 vests are worn over the LBEs and the RBA. The M-16A2s use 550-cord and tape to modify the slings. The magazine, visible on the right, has a loop made of the same cord and is wedged into the bottom of it and secured with tape. This loop enabled Rangers to pull the magazines out of the tightly packed ammunition pouches. (Anton Berendsen)

We were told that the reaction forces were on the way. The Little Birds continued to do gun runs and to fire rockets. They kept our spirits up. Floyd and I were pulling guard on the window that we climbed through to enter the courtyard. An RPG was shot at us. The location where the RPG came from was marked with a tracer and blown up with a rocket. After that, the RPG fire tapered off. I kept looking at my watch wondering where the reaction force was. I was praying a lot for all of us. The firing from the enemy lulled a little bit. We found a spigot and we started doing a water resupply by putting canteens on a stick and passing them through the window next door to where the casualties were. This particular water resupply wasn't taught in Ranger School, that's for damn sure.

At about 04:00 the reaction forces finally linked up with us. We gave the Ranger running password. At about 05:45 they had finally recovered the bodies at the crash site. We were told that there wasn't enough room in the APCs for us. Therefore we would be exfilling by foot, that's when the Mogadishu 500 began. It was a mad dash for our lives. The sun was up and thus began a new day in the Mog. We started to move with the APCs next to us trying to provide cover. Fire was coming from everywhere. The APCs took off and left us — that sucked. Bullets started hitting all around us. I remember I felt something hit my arm and knock me back. I looked over and there was a gash in my BDU, knocking the American flag off my arm. The same bullet that grazed me hit Sgt Ramaglia in the side, taking out a good chunk of meat. I told him he was hit and for him not to worry about it. We crossed the street and continued the Mog 500. Gunfire was coming from everywhere. We passed a 5-ton truck that had been blown up. There was blood all over the streets. We kept pushing on. We turned a corner and there were two tanks sitting in the road, what a sight. We all got under cover near the tanks. Nearby was a tan Humvee that had 'security police' written on the side. A guy was in the turret. The guy got shot in the neck. One of the tanks fired a round at the building where the gunfire came from. The entire building was leveled. I thought 'holy shit.' We started moving again and saw APCs leaving. I thought 'here we go again.' We yelled at the APCs, but they wouldn't stop. Some of the guys had gotten on the APCs but there were about 25 of us who could not. We were running alongside of the APCs for about another 2 blocks before they stopped. We piled on them and got the hell out of there.

We drove to the Pakistani [controlled] Stadium, got out at the stadium and shook everyone's hands. By the way, the Pakistanis and Malaysians were the ones in the APCs that got us out [The Pakistanis provided 4 tanks during the early part of the relief convoy only]. The casualties were evacuated to the hospitals.

We then found out who had been killed during the mission. The mood was somber. We ate some food and were flown back to our hanger. It had been 18 hours since we had left. Everyone soaked up what had happened.

There was a memorial the next day. Many tears were shed and many more will be for the ones that we lost. I know this event has forever changed my life.

Fighting in the mountains – Afghanistan

Since October 2001, the 75th Ranger Regiment has deployed its battalions to spearhead the campaign against Taliban and al Qaeda fighters in Afghanistan and Pakistan. Rangers conducted several nighttime low-level combat parachute assaults onto Taliban facilities in southern Afghanistan. Not since the Japanese in World War II have Americans fought such a deadly and dedicated enemy. The fighters are battle-hardened veterans and many have been at war since the Soviet invasion of Afghanistan in 1979. Thousands of fighters are lodged in the inaccessible mountains.

The Battle of Takur Ghar (Executive Summary, DOD, May 24, 2002)

On March 4, 2002, Rangers and other US special operations forces were involved in missions against al Qaeda and Taliban forces holed up in the Shah-e-Kot valley, southeast of Gardez.

US commanders wanted to insert special operators for reconnaissance missions on the crest of the mountain. The 10,000-foot mountain range was ideal for this maneuvre but al-Qaeda forces, unbeknownst to US military intelligence, already had a position in the area.

A MH-47E helicopter from the 2nd Battalion, 160th Special Operations Aviation Regiment (Airborne) was to airlift SEALs (Sea, Air and Land naval commandos) to the mountaintop. As they prepared to land, the pilots spotted fresh tracks, and the chopper was immediately struck by an RPG and small arms fire, cutting the hydraulic and oil lines. As the crippled helicopter maneuvred to vacate, one SEAL lost his footing and fell approximately 5–10 feet to the ground. The helicopter eventually crash-landed about seven kilometers away.

Another helicopter picked up the personnel from the crashed aircraft and returned to base at Gardez. Some time later, the same helicopter and SEALs returned to retrieve their missing comrade. The helicopter took fire, and although damaged was able to successfully deliver the team. On the ground the team came under fire, resulting in the death of AF combat controller (CCT) John Chapman and two SEALs being wounded. A QRF (Quick Reaction Force), comprised of Rangers from the 1st Battalion, 75th Ranger Regiment at Gardez, was requested as an AC-130 SPECTRE gunship provided covering fire for the team's withdrawal down the mountain.

The 23-man QRF team loaded onto two MH-47E helicopters and headed to the area. "Razor 01" carried 10 Rangers, an enlisted tactical air controller, a combat controller and a Pararescueman. "Razor 02" transported 10 Rangers. In an ironic twist of fate, the most technologically sophisticated special operations force in the world was unable to effectively communicate with their various elements. The exact location of the SEAL team could not be established. The Rangers inserted in the same location where the first helicopter had come under fire, not

knowing much about the dozen or so well entrenched al Qaeda guerrillas.

As the helicopter, Razor 01, attempted to land in the daylight, it was shot down with RPGs and heavy machinegun fire. The door gunner, Army SGT Phil Svitak, was killed by an AK-47 round and both pilots were wounded as they crash-landed. Rangers Brad Crose, Matt Commons and Marc Anderson survived the initial ambush but were killed as they attempted to exit the aircraft. Still en route, Razor 02 was diverted to a safe area for further instructions and would later drop off the Ranger chalk and one SEAL 800 meters east and 2000 feet below the now downed chopper. Eventually, the SEAL would link up with the SEAL team infiltrating the mountain and the Rangers would struggle up the snow-covered range to join their beleaguered comrades. It would take them two hours.

As back up was slowly making its way to them, the soldiers at the crash-site consolidated and attempted a limited assault on the enemy, calling in airstrikes to within 50 meters of their own position. By 0700 hours they were no longer in danger of being overrun.

The Rangers from Razor 02 established link-up at the crashed helicopter by 1030 but still had to defeat the enemy controlling the top of the hill, a mere 50 meters from their position. With the arrival of the ten men of Razor 02, the Rangers prepared to assault the enemy bunkers. As the Air Force CCT called in a last air-strike on the enemy bunkers and with two machineguns providing suppression fire, seven Rangers stormed the hill in the knee-deep snow, shooting and throwing grenades. Within minutes, the Rangers took the hill, killing several al Qaeda. Chapman's body was recovered in a bunker, and fifteen feet away, the body of Navy SEAL Neil Roberts was also retrieved. The Rangers undertook to consolidate at the top of the mountain. The Rangers, Army crewmembers, and Air Force personnel began moving the wounded up the steep slope, four to six men carrying each casualty. Al Qaeda guerillas on another ridgeline about 400 meters away fired on the team's makeshift aid station. Air Force Pararescueman Jason Cunningham was hit and eventually died from his wounds.

The 75th Ranger Regiment is the tip of the spearhead of America's special operations. In the ongoing war against terrorism, the Rangers have participated in several combat parachute assaults, as well as many still classified operations, most notably in Afghanistan. Ranger Marc Anderson is laid to rest with military honors. He is one of five Rangers that has been killed in action. (Jeff Zika)

The Ranger Assault Carrying Kit (RACK) will accept all MOLLE compatible pockets. The RACK was designed for the members of the 75th Ranger Regiment. It frees up the hip and abdomen area by being worn on the chest, thus not conflicting with a waist belt on a rucksack. The RACK can be worn over body armor. (Specialty Plastics)

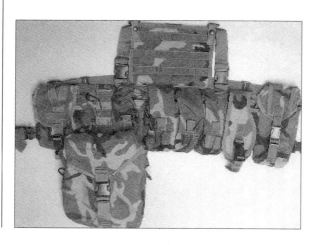

The trapped men waited for a night extraction. The enemy defenses around Takur Ghar were too intense to try another daylight rescue. Throughout the day, observation posts on adjoining hilltops, manned by Australian and American SOF, called in fire on al Qaeda forces attempting to reinforce the mountaintop. A total of eight helicopters, including five Apaches, had been damaged or destroyed resulting in the Marine Corps providing Cobra gunship support.

At about 2015, four helicopters from the 160th SOAR extracted the Rangers on Takur Ghar as well as the SEALs further down the mountainside. Seven Americans were killed in battle and 11 were wounded.

The MOLLE (Modular Lightweight Load-carrying Equipment) System is a joint service item, designed and developed to incorporate the requirements of the Army and Marines and was designed to replace the All-purpose Lightweight Individual Carrying Equipment (ALICE). It consists of a modular rucksack with removable compartments and components, and a fighting load vest with removable pouch configurations. It is disliked both by Rangers and Marines. (Sarah Underhill, US Army)

"Razor 01," an MH-47E Chinook helicopter, sits atop Takur Ghar, the site of a battle between US special operations forces and al Qaeda fighters during Operation Anaconda in March, 2002. (DOD)

BIBLIOGRAPHY

Adkin, Mark Major, *Urgent Fury The Battle for Grenada,* Lexington Books, New York, 1989

Altieri, James T., *Darby's Rangers*, Ranger Book Committee, Arnold, MO, 1977

Altieri, James T., *The Spearheaders*, Zenger Publishing Company, Washington, DC, 1979

Bahmanyar, Mir, *Darby's Ranger 1942–44: Onward we Stagger*, Osprey Publishing Ltd, Oxford, 2003

Bass, Robert D., *Swamp Fox,* Sandlapper Publishing Company, Orangeburg, SC, 1989

Black, Robert W., *Rangers in Korea*, Ivy Books, New York, 1989

Black, Robert W., *Rangers in World War II*, Ivy Books, New York, 1992

Bolger, Daniel P., *Death Ground Today's American Infantry in Battle*, Presidio Press, Novato, CA, 1999

Bowden, Mark, *Black Hawk Down*, Atlantic Monthly Press, New York, 1999

Breuer, William, *The Great Raid on Cabanatuan,* John Wiley & Sons, New York, 1994

Breuer, William B., *Operation Torch*, St Martins Press, New York, 1985

Burford, John, *LRRPs in Action,* Squadron/Signal Publications, Carrollton, TX, 1994

Callahan & North, *Daniel Morgan, Ranger of the Revolution*, AMS Press, New York, 1973

Cuneo, John R., *Robert Rogers of the Rangers*, Richardson & Steirmna, New York, 1987

Darby, William & Baumer, William, *We Led the Way: Darby's Rangers*, Presidio Press, San Rafael, CA, 1980

Delauter, Jr., Roger U., *McNeill's Rangers*, H.E. Howard, Appomattox, VA, 1986

Delong, Kent & Tuckey, Steven, *Mogadishu! Heroism and Tragedy*, Praeger, Westport, CT, 1994

Field, Ron "Ranger: Behind Enemy Lines in Vietnam," *Military Illustrated*, London, 2000

Flanagan, Edward M. Lt. Gen., *Battle for Panama, Inside Operation Just Cause*, Brassey's US Inc., New York, 1993

Foley, Dennis, *Special Men, A LRP's Recollection*, Ivy Books, New York,1994

Hogan, Jr., David W., *Raiders or Elite Infantry? The Changing Role of the US Army Rangers from Dieppe to Grenada*, Greenwood Press, Westport, CT, 1992

Hopkins, James E.T. & Jones, John M., *Spearhead A Complete History of Merrill's Marauder Rangers*, Galahad Press, Baltimore, MD, 1999

Hunter, Charles Newton, *Galahad*, The Naylor Company, San Antonio, TX, 1963

Ingersoll, Ralph, Captain, *The Battle is the Pay-off*, Harcourt Brace & Co., New York, 1943

Jones, Virgil C., *Ranger Mosby*, EPM Publications, Reston, VA, 1987

King, Michael J. Dr., *Leavenworth Papers: Rangers, Selected Combat Operations in World War II*, Combat Studies Institute, Fort Leavenworth, KS, 1985

Ladd, James, *Commandos and Rangers of World War II*, St Martins Press, New York, 1978

Landau Alan M. & Landau Freida W., *Airborne Rangers*, Motorbooks International, St. Paul, MN, 1992

Lane, Ronald L., *Rudder's Rangers*, Ranger Associates, Manassas, VA, 1979

Lanning, Michael Lee, *Inside the LRRPs, Rangers in Vietnam*, Ivy Books, New York, 1988

Linderer, Gary, *Six Silent Men, Book 3*, Ivy Books, New York, 1997

Linderer, Gary, *Eyes Behind the Lines*, Ivy Books, New York, 1991

Linderer, Gary, *The Eyes of the Eagle*, Ivy Books, New York, 1991

Lock, John D. Major, *To Fight with Intrepidity ...*, Pocket, New York, 1998

Loescher, Burt, *The History of Rogers Rangers, Vols I-III*, Self-published, 1946, 1969, 1957 Burlingame, CA,

Martinez, Reynel, *Six Silent Men, Book 1*, Ivy Books, New York, 1997

McConnell, Malcolm, *Just Cause*, St Martin's Press, New York, 1991

McRaven, William H., *Spec Ops*, Presidio Press, Novato, CA, 1995

Miller, Kenneth, *Six Silent Men, Book 2*, Ivy Books, New York, 1997

Mosby, John S., *The Memoirs of Colonel John S. Mosby*, J. S. Sanders & Co, Nashville, TN, 1995

Nadel, Joel & Wright, J.R., *Special Men and Special Missions*, Greenhill Books, London, 1994

Ogburn, Jr., Charlton, *The Marauders*, Harper, New York, 1959

Padden, Ian, *US Rangers*, Bantam Books, New York, 1985

Rottman, Gordon L., *Panama 1989-90*, Osprey Publishing Ltd, London, 1991

Rottman, Gordon L., *US Army Combat Equipments 1910-88*, Osprey Publishing Ltd, London, 1989

Rottman, Gordon L., *US Army Rangers & LRRP Units 1942-87*, Osprey Publishing Ltd, London, 1987

Ericson, Don & Rotundo John, *Charlie Rangers*, Ivy Books, New York, 1989

Russell, Lee E. & Mendez, M. Albert, *Grenada 1983*, Osprey Publishing Ltd, London, 1983

Schauer, Hartmut, *US Rangers*, Motorbuch Verlag, Stuttgart, 1992

Seagrave, Gordon S., *The Burma Surgeon Returns*, W.W. Norton and Co., New York, 1943

Shapiro, Milton, *Ranger Battalion, American Rangers in World War II*, Julian Messner, New York, 1979

Stanton, Shelby, *Rangers at War, LRRPs in Vietnam*, Ivy Books, New York, 1992

Taylor, Thomas H. Col, *Rangers Lead the Way*, Turner Publishing Company, Paducah, KY, 1996

US Army, *Merrill's Marauders*, Center of Military History, US Army, Washington, DC, 1944

US Army, *Small Unit Actions*, Center of Military History, US Army, Washington, DC, 1982

Walker, Greg, *At the Hurricane's Eye*, Ivy Books, New York, 1994

Watts, Joe C., *Korean Nights The 4th Ranger Infantry Company Abn 1950-1951*, Southern Heritage Press, St. Petersburg, FL, 1997

Wert, Jeffry D., *Mosby's Rangers*, Simon & Schuster, New York, 1990

Zedric, Lance Q. & Dilley, Michael F. *Elite Warriors 300: Years of America's Best Fighting Troops*, Pathfinder Publishing, Ventura, CA, 1996

GLOSSARY

5307th Composite Unit Provisional	Famous WWII long range patrolling unit known as "Merrill's Marauders."
Advanced Individual Training (AIT)	Most Rangers take this four-week infantry course right after BASIC training.
Airborne School	Three-week course to teach the principles of parachuting at Fort Benning, Georgia.
Airborne-shuffle	A slow and steady jog.
Basic training	An eight-week course which teaches the recruit basic soldiering skills.
Battboy	A Ranger whose first unit is a Ranger battalion. Graduates of Ranger School who come to a Ranger battalion after having served in another unit are not considered Battboys.
Blood wings	An initiation ceremony after successful completion of Airborne School.
High-and-tight	The distinctive Ranger haircut, a very short, modified Mohawk.
Hooah	Supposedly derived from a Native American greeting, it means everything and anything. Tone is very important.
Koalifying	Hanging upside down from a tree or telephone pole.
Line-dogs	Regular Ranger infantrymen.
Little birds	MH/AH 6 Helicopters.
LRRP/LRP	Long range units made famous during the Vietnam War.
Maggots	A Ranger who carries heavy weapons systems.
Pre-Ranger	A three-week course for Battboys prior to attending Ranger School

Ranger Creed

Ranger Philosophy; the first letters in each stanza will spell Ranger:

Recognizing that I volunteered as a Ranger, fully knowing the hazards of my chosen profession, I will always endeavor to uphold the prestige, honor, and high esprit de corps of my Ranger Regiment.

Acknowledging the fact that a Ranger is a more elite soldier who arrives at the cutting edge of battle by land, sea, or air, I accept the fact that as a Ranger my country expects me to move farther, faster and fight harder than any other soldier.

Never shall I fail my comrades. I will always keep myself mentally alert, physically strong and morally straight and I will shoulder more than my share of the task whatever it may be. One-hundred-percent and then some.

Gallantly will I show the world that I am a specially selected and well-trained soldier. My courtesy to superior officers, neatness of dress and care of equipment shall set the example for others to follow.

Energetically will I meet the enemies of my country. I shall defeat them on the field of battle for I am better trained and will fight with all my might. Surrender is not a Ranger word. I will never leave a fallen comrade to fall into the hands of the enemy and under no circumstances will I ever embarrass my country.

Readily will I display the intestinal fortitude required to fight on to the Ranger objective and complete the mission though I be the lone survivor.

Ranger Handbook
The bible for all Rangers. Tactics, planning and survival skills are listed in this manual.

Ranger Indoctrination Program (RIP)	Three-week course designed to weed out the weak, Ranger wannabes.
Ranger Orientation Program (ROP)	Three-week course designed to re-orient the Ranger-qualified soldier prior to his return to a Ranger unit.
Ranger School	A leadership school lasting 58 days.
Ranger Scroll	The 75th Ranger Regiment's distinctive unit patch adopted from the famous Darby Rangers.
Ranger Tab	The patch worn by graduates of Ranger School.
Ranger Training Brigade	The unit responsible for running Ranger School.
Ready Reaction Force (RRF) 1	A state of high alert for a Ranger battalion.
Rippies	Students attending RIP.
Robert Rogers	Famous colonial Ranger who wrote 28 Rules of Discipline from which the Rangers' Standing Orders are derived.
Roger's Standing Orders	These are 19 stanzas imparting Ranger wisdom.
Smoke session	Grueling physical exercises designed to test a soldier's mental toughness.
Sua Sponte	The official motto of the Ranger Regiment. Derived from the long history of members being volunteers. The Latin term means "of their own accord."
Tabless bitch	A Ranger who successfully passed RIP and is waiting to attend Ranger School. This term pertains to 75th Rangers only.

MUSEUMS

National Infantry Museum, Building 396, Baltzell Avenue, Fort Benning, Georgia

Rogers Island Visitors Center,
PO Box 208 - 11 Rogers Island Drive,
Fort Edward,
NY 12828

Rogers Island, which is listed on the National Register of Historic Sites, was the home base for Robert Rogers and his Rangers from 1756–59.

Author's website:
www.suasponte.com

COLOR PLATE COMMENTARY

A: INVASION OF GRENADA, 1983

1. During one of the follow-on missions in Grenada, Rangers were airlifted by US Marine Corps CH-46s. As they neared their objective they came under heavy fire, and one helicopter crash-landed. Several Rangers nearly drowned and were ordered to drop rucks as they scrambled out of the partially submerged chopper. This man wears the Vietnam-era OG 107 (olive green, Army shade 107) jungle fatigues. His patrol cap was lost and his Ranger "high-and-tight" hair cut is clearly visible. The Ranger carries the M-16A1 rifle and load bearing equipment (LBE).

2. The 1st Battalion (Ranger), 75th Infantry Scroll. The colors red, black and white are adopted from the 1st Ranger Battalion founded during World War II, the Darby Rangers. The shape is more reminiscent of the various scrolls created during the Vietnam War by Long Range and Ranger units.

3. 2nd Battalion Scroll. This unit was founded several months after the 1st Battalion.

4. The M-67 90mm recoilless rifle. An excellent anti-armor weapon, however it is difficult to carry in the bush. These weapons destroyed several armored personnel carriers at Point Salines, Grenada.

B: RANGER, B/CO., 3/75, PANAMA, 1989

1. The newly created 75th Ranger Regiment deployed in its entirety to participate in Operation Just Cause, the invasion of Panama, in 1989. Wearing the lightweight rip-stop woodland pattern battle dress uniform (BDU) with Load Bearing Equipment (LBE), this man is weighed down by the large ALICE rucksack, probably loaded up with extra ammunition. His personal weapon is the M-16A2. His Fritz Kevlar helmet carries additional strips of shredded BDU material on its top, partly as a means of recognition for friendly forces.

2. The M-16A2 is yet another variant of the M-16 and entered service with the Ranger regiment during the mid 1980s. The A2 variant features a three round burst when placed on automatic.

3. The 75th Ranger Regiment reverted to the World War II Ranger Battalion Scrolls. There are four distinct versions: one for each battalion and one for members of the Regimental Headquarters and Headquarters Company.

4. This set of load bearing equipment represents the standard way in which it was assembled per Regimental Standard Operating Procedure (RSOP). Note that each item is tied to the belt with parachute cord (550 cord) and that the metal hooks and canteen cups are covered with tape.

5. The regimental SOP for camouflaging the face is a tiger stripe pattern, possibly in tribute to the Vietnam Rangers who wore tiger stripe camouflage uniforms.

C: RANGER, BRAVO COMPANY, 3/75, OPERATION DESERT STORM, 1991

1. Wearing the 3-pattern desert camouflage uniform, this man's Kevlar camouflage cover is of the 6-pattern variety.

2. The M-16A2 sling is modified to make it more functional when fast-roping from a Black Hawk helicopter. Tape and 550 cord secure the sling. The magazine has a loop made of 550 cord and is wedged into the magazine, then secured with tape. This loop allows Rangers to withdraw a fresh magazine more easily.

3. The Ranger Body Armor (RBA) was specifically manufactured for this mission, and was designed by the US Army Natick Research Center to meet the operational needs of the 75th Ranger Regiment. It consists of two parts, a flexible vest and a rigid plate. Weighing approximately 8lb (medium size), the vest consists of a Kevlar filler encased in a nylon woodland camouflage carrier and protects the front and back torso from most 9mm and 44 magnum threats. The 8lb ceramic upgrade plate, which provides front torso coverage, is made of 2 x 2 in. aluminum oxide ceramic tiles. When the upgrade plate is inserted into the front pocket of the vest, it protects an area approximately 10 x 12 in. from 5.56mm and 7.62mm ball projectiles.

4. Some Rangers wrote their blood type on their desert boots.

5. Note the patch with Stars facing forward (as per US Flag protocol) was worn on the right shoulder.

D: RANGER, AFGHANISTAN, 2002

1. This is a hypothetical representation of a Ranger fighting in Afghanistan in 2002. He wears the Modular/Integrated Communications Helmet (MICH), which has been in use since 2001–02, when it replaced the "Fritz" Kevlar helmet. It has a 3-pattern cover and the attachment device for his third generation Night Optical Device (7-Series). The MICH is a single modular headgear system that provides ballistic, fragmentation, aural and impact protection, while being night vision, communications and Nuclear, Biological and Chemical (NBC) equipment-compatible. It is part of the SPEAR (Special Operations Forces Personnel Equipment Advanced Requirements) program. SPEAR is designed to improve personal equipment, tailoring to the particular needs of special operations forces. The internal headset may be worn alone or with the helmet. He wears a new generation Ranger Body Armor with a variety of MOLLE and RACK pouches. The modern Ranger is allowed a tremendous amount of flexibility with his personal gear as long as it makes tactical sense. Note his camouflage painted knee and elbow pads and mountain boots.

2. The M-4 carbine entered service with the Ranger regiment in the late 1990s and although an upgraded version has entered special operations in 2002, the M-4 remains the standard weapon for the Rangers.

3. ACOG 4X Scope.

4. Forward handgrip

5. Rail Interface System (RIS) for accessory attachments.

6. AN-PEQ-2 IR (Infra-Red) Pointer/Illuminator.

7. In 2001, the 75th Ranger Regiment adopted a tan beret and designed new flashes. The colors of the flash (white, green, blue, orange, khaki, and red) represent the six original combat team colors of Merrill's Marauders. The red stripes on each border of the flash identify the wearer as to which battalion he belongs: one stripe for 1st Battalion; two for 2nd Battalion; and three for 3rd Battalion. Members of the Headquarters and Headquarters Company, 75th Ranger Regiment, have a plain black border with no stripe. The colors of the shield (blue, white, red, and green)

represent four of the original six combat teams of the 5307th Composite Unit (Provisional), commonly referred to as "Merrill's Marauders," which were identified by color. To avoid confusion, the other two colors, khaki and orange were not represented in the design; however, khaki was represented by the color of the uniform worn by the United States in the China-Burma-India Theater during World War II. The unit's close cooperation with the Chinese forces in the China-Burma-India Theater is represented by the sun symbol from the Chinese flag. The white star represents the Star of Burma, the country in which the Marauders campaigned during World War II. The lightning bolt is symbolic of the strike characteristics of the Marauders behind-the-line activities.

E: INDOCTRINATION, 1980s

1. "Hazing" is a part of becoming a Ranger. In this scenario a tabbed (Ranger School graduate) Ranger "smokes" a newbie, a tabless or Scrolled Ranger. Ranger push-ups are always elevated. This young Ranger's muscles will eventually fail him and bring him down in a rather uncontrolled manner. In his turn, he will attend and graduate Ranger School and continue the tradition of hazing.

2. One Ranger is "koalifying," while another does elevated push-ups from the same telephone pole.

3. This scene represents the Ranger Indoctrination Program on Day One from the mid to late 1980s. The Cadre member is wearing the now outdated OG 107s, and the young recruits are exercising as part of the rigorous daily physical training.

F: FAST ROPING

One of the most commonly used insertion techniques for special operations personnel, fast roping was used during operations against Somali warlords in Mogadishu in 1993. Accounts vividly describe the "brown-outs," when the rotor blades of the powerful Back Hawk helicopters kicked up dirt and debris, including loose roofs and sometimes people too. Hovering long enough to get the Rangers down the ropes was often extremely difficult. Fast roping is not as easy as it may appear, as heavy personal gear can make for a somewhat hard and uncontrolled landing. Occasionally, one Ranger will land on top of another. Both hands and feet are used when fast roping to slow down the descent.

G: ASSAULT ON RIO HATO, PANAMA, DECEMBER 1989

The 2nd and 3rd Ranger Battalions conducted a parachute assault onto Rio Hato, Panama, in December 1989. The mission was a great success, despite the time it took to assemble enough men to launch the attacks.

1. This Ranger jumped a T-10 parachute and is entangled in a tree. His weapon was secured in the M-1950 weapons carrying container, so he has to resort to grenades to eliminate the immediate threat to his life.

2. and 3. Panamanian Defense Forces are equipped with US uniforms and equipment. Many disappeared into the night wearing civilian clothing.

4. Most of the C-130s used during the parachute drop were hit by enemy fire. Rio Hato was manned by two elite companies, but resistance was minimal.

H: MOGADISHU, OCTOBER 1993

Rangers from B/Co, 3/75 fight their way through multiple ambushes in the labyrinth of Mogadishu, Somalia, October 3, 1993. Fortunately, Rangers wore body armor and it saved many lives. Although the majority of small arms used by the Somali gunmen were 7.62 caliber, their aim was not too accurate as vividly detailed here, and Ranger casualties were reasonably light. As the Ranger convoy became confused en route back to a shot down Black Hawk, Somalis were able to run from position to position and successfully engaged the Rangers in many ambushes.

1. Most Somali gunmen tended to simply point their weapons in the general vicinity of the enemy and spray bullets. Weapons were commonplace and every household owned at least one, if not several automatic guns.

During street battles with UN and US troops, Somalis were able to navigate easily through the maze of Mogadishu streets. The Somali fighters would follow the convoy and, often, overtake it to set up ambush after ambush

2. The Humvees are Kevlar armored. An MK-19 automatic grenade launcher and .50 caliber machine gun are visible.

3. The Rangers wear 3-pattern and 6-pattern desert camouflage uniforms. In many instances the Ranger body armor worn underneath their LBEs proved to be a life saver, although Rangers did die of 7.62mm wounds as only a small portion of the front had a ceramic plate to protect against that particular caliber of bullet.

INDEX